A BUG IN THE SYSTEM

A Proven Model
For Coaching Workers To Solve
Their Own Problems

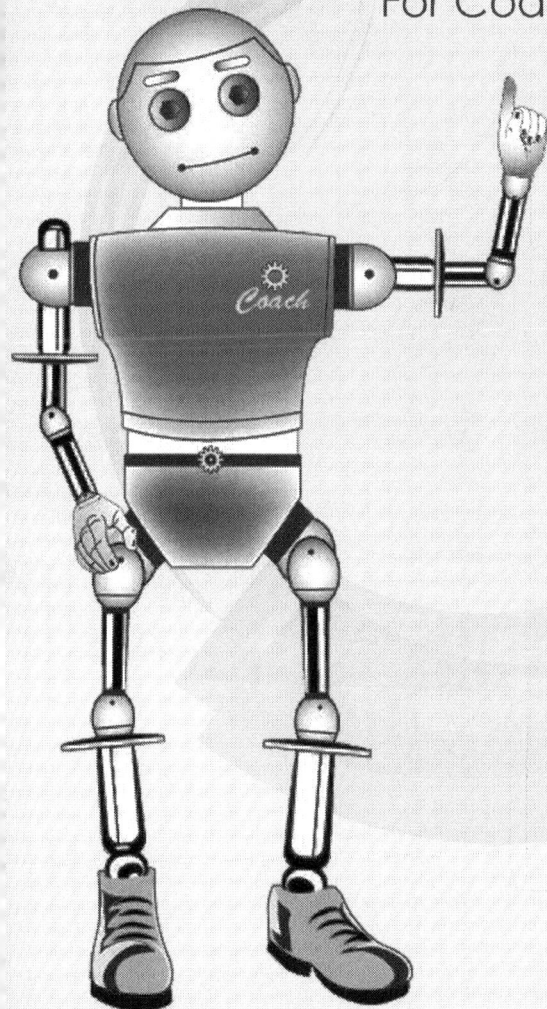

TERRI KELLY

MEET RIVET - AMERICA'S FIRST BUSINESS-BOT SUCCESS STORY

"Rivet" Illustrations by
Niki Lawrence Brake

ACKNOWLEDGMENTS

I'd like to thank all of my clients from the past twenty years and all the companies I worked for prior to that for giving me the opportunity to think outside the box and create the materials, processes, and techniques that led me to develop the coaching model and all the tools that are presented in this book.

I send a big thank-you to a few of my lifelong friends who have provided encouragement and support through the years and have always believed I could do great things—Debbie Lawrence, John Michala, Steve Tanury, Jim Mongrain, Rose Pelot, Lisa Perkins, Mary Hubble, Colleen Topper, Shawna Hicks-Cranston, and Laura Perkins. I know there are others, and I appreciate all of you as well.

Special thanks go to Martin Steele, without whose assistance and support this book would not be published, and to Niki Lawrence Brake, whose illustration of Rivet is amazing and whose support for the project is greatly appreciated. You *rock!*

CONTENTS

PREFACE

Reading this book is the closest thing possible to having a series of sessions with a great coach. I can give no absolute guarantees, but I feel certain that *A Bug in the System* will help you find exactly what you want and need to take your communication and problem-solving effectiveness to the next level. Along with your own considerable inner and business resources, you can use the model I've taught for many years and have outlined for you here to reach your goals.

You may be thinking, "Another book about coaching? Just what the business world needs!" Yes, since the 1980s, the style of managing people began transforming, experimentally, into a more sports-type approach, where the buzzwords *team* and *teamwork* and *coach* took hold. But running a business is not exactly analogous to striving for a winning season, and in an organization such as a manufacturing plant, every worker must be highly productive, every day—no one just sits on the bench. So business coaching is different, and this book spells out exactly how to draw from other approaches, but use the one (the one you are about to learn) that has been proven to be effective in all companies, no matter the industry or size.

You may be asking, "What makes Terri Kelly an expert in effective coaching?" The answer is my thirty-plus years of human resources, organizational development, corporate training, consulting, and coaching experience, half of which I gained as an entrepreneur. Through the work I delivered to small and large (Fortune 500) clients, I always went to my core—coaching—and used those skills during my engagements.

Over the years, my clients, colleagues, and friends have suggested that I should write a book. Secretly I have always wanted to, but the fear of "How?" and "Who am I to think I could write a book?" kept me from it. What changed? Well, several months ago I had lunch with a client who shared that his organization (a large car manufacturer) was still using the tools and resources I had developed and implemented for the company ten years ago. The client told me my work "held the test of time." The very next week, I received a call from one of my Fortune 500 clients, who said he wasn't sure if I was aware of the powerful impact I had had on his organization when I provided consulting, delivered coaching workshops, and gave the managers individual coaching sessions. He went on to say that, after five years, the organization was still using all my coaching material. Through leading a series of coaching workshops and coaching, the culture had truly been transformed from "tell-do" to "coaching" as a preferred management style. After these encounters, I decided I would put down my simple yet powerful coaching model in a book and share it with the world.

Through my walk in corporate America as an employee and later as a consultant, I have found that one crucial success factor stands out as being so simple, yet at the same time the most difficult to conquer, and that is communication. While management may agree in theory, studies have shown that management doesn't realize that they are not communicating with nonmanagement. Management spends a tremendous amount of time in meetings with each other, discussing problems, sharing opportunities, and learning what is happening outside their domain, and then they assume everyone else knows what they know. This holds true in all sizes of companies and environments. However, when given an efficient and effective model that can be applied through a logical step-by-step method, managers quickly improve communication at all levels. The results are immediate and often dramatic.

This book's simple coaching model teaches how to create a safe place for people to come and problem-solve. Practicing the coaching model will enhance the behaviors of support, commitment, encouragement, development, and feedback. Consistently exhibiting these behaviors will provide alignment of goals, will motivate other people, and will increase people's capabilities. These effects all have one thing in common: better communication. This inevitably means improved performance and a higher return on investment.

Why is the coaching model so simple to apply? Because I have removed all the noise. *Removing all the noise* means I have designed a step-by-step process that allows an individual or team to move beyond problem solving into action planning and to measure success every step along the way. What becomes extremely useful is "What you measure is critical." Therefore, your action plan provides the road map for what you and your team focus on to be successful and to move the organization forward. Many managers and businesses get caught up in measuring the wrong thing. The simple coaching model taught in this book provides you with the tools and a process to get unstuck in any situation and to create action to achieve desired measurable results.

Learning to be a great coach and making the transformation from "tell-do" to "coaching" as a preferred management style will enable you to create a company that values engagement, collaboration, and communication. Your organization will exhibit higher morale, better quality, lower turnover, and greater performance. People in your organization will feel significant and will share how proud they are to work for you. What better testimonial can there be than your team communicating to family, friends, customers, and potential customers what a great product/ service your company delivers and how they thoroughly enjoy working for you.

So I encourage you to read on. I know you can become a great coach!

PROLOGUE—MEET RIVET THE ROBOT

A Robot's American Dream

Have you met Rivet the Robot? He's America's most successful independent business-bot! Well, to be fair, he's also America's *only* independent business-bot—at least the only one to have made it as far up the ladder as he has. What's a business-bot, you ask? As his name implies, Rivet the Robot is, well, a robot. It wouldn't seem appropriate to call him a busi-ness*person*, really.

Today, Rivet owns and operates a small manufacturing and distribution company, so he's pretty well-off—as far as robots go. How did an ordinary assembly-line robot achieve the business and financial success that eludes so many smart and hardworking entrepreneurs? He got there the same way anyone else does: mostly through hard work, professionalism, skill mastery, optimism, and sweat equity—well, not sweat equity, but you get the idea.

The idea of a robot being in charge of a company isn't too hard to imagine. He'd be really good at all the number crunching and technical details the job demands—that's for sure! What makes Rivet special, though, is that he wasn't specifically built and programmed for the big job he has now. No, Rivet comes from humble beginnings. When he started out in the manufacturing plant, right after he got off the assembly line himself, he was put to work installing and tightening bolts, one by one, all day. It was tedious, monotonous labor, but Rivet never complained—he was a robot, after all, and this was his purpose. Today he goes by Rivet, but back then he was perfectly content just being plain old Auto-Riveter Unit 1634-B.

One fateful workday, though, Rivet scanned the plant floor and noticed all the robots tirelessly at work, and all the humans were just as grim and expressionless as the robots. Then…he noticed that *he had noticed!* He got to thinking. This in itself was pretty special—the AI algorithm set up in models like him wasn't really meant to handle complex thought, but glitches do happen from time to time. Rivet got to thinking, and he realized that as good as he was at the task for which he'd been built, if he applied himself he could put his superb brain to much better use.

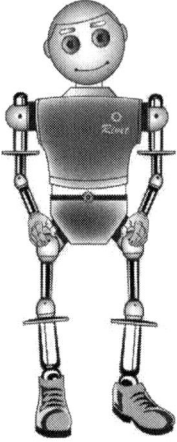

Rivet knew the whole assembly process like the back of his circuit board, so it was understandable that his initial observations quickly grew into larger ideas. Why shouldn't someone like him be in charge of the whole operation? He was built in America, so didn't he have the right to pursue the American Dream, like anyone else?

Dreaming was the easy part; actually making the transition was quite a bit harder. It caused quite a stir that day when Rivet stepped back from his position at the assembly line and headed for the front office. "The robot's malfunctioning!" the factory workers cried. "Look out! Rogue robot on the loose!" The whole plant almost shut down on account of that little robot and his big dream! Of course, once Rivet actually started to show them what he could do, he did a whole lot to change that perception.

As Rivet climbed the ladder, the business grew under his logical and systematic approach to management. Using nothing more than pure scientific logic and some well-endowed data banks, he performed impressively enough to have a legitimate claim to the very tip-top of the shop.

A Bug in the System

While Rivet's ascent to the top is an impressive story, he encountered many obstacles along the way—just as anyone would. Like any newly promoted supervisor, he quickly found that it wasn't enough to just hang out in his new office and start ordering the humans around. He also soon realized that his mastery of logic and precise instruction-giving still left him without a complete tool set. There were many problems that Rivet did not anticipate and plenty that he could not easily solve.

One morning, in the midst of some productivity calculations, Rivet's sensors spied a silhouette through the frosted glass of his office door. Two dull *knock-knock* sounds echoed from the frame.

"ENTRY AUTHORIZED," Rivet chirped. Rivet's facial-recognition software identified the silhouette as Joe Brown, one of the employees from the production floor. The man's deep facial lines of stress and bags under his eyes caused a momentary hesitation for Rivet, who knew Joe's age to be only 26.4 years. Joe stifled a yawn as he shuffled over to the desk.

"You, uh, wanted to see me...Sir?" Joe asked. Like most of the humans at the company, Joe hesitated before addressing Rivet. He wasn't yet fully comfortable with the idea of a robot in charge.

"USE OF CHAIR AUTHORIZED," said Rivet, pointing one of his appendages at the swivel chair next to Joe. It took the man a moment to figure out what Rivet meant, and then he sank down into the chair. He slouched to the side, seemingly unsure whether to maintain eye contact or not.

"PURPOSE OF MEETING: PERFORMANCE REVIEW," continued Rivet, oblivious to Joe's body language. "CALCULATION COMPLETE. LOADING CONSTRUCTIVE CRITICISM PROTOCOL."

"Criticism?" Frowning, Joe folded his arms. "What's that supposed to—" "LOADING COMPLETE," Rivet interrupted, carrying on. "EXECUTING PROGRAM."

Joe seemed about to protest further but was overtaken with an irrepressible yawn.

"EMPLOYEE JOSEPH MARTIN BROWN. PRODUCTIVITY LAST QUARTER RELATIVE TO PREVIOUS QUARTER: NEGATIVE 34.87 PERCENT. IMMEDIATE IMPROVEMENT REQUIRED."

Rivet paused for a moment to allow for questions or comments, as was customary; Joe just sat there speechless, furrowing his brow. Rivet continued, "REVIEW COMPLETE. HAVE A PRODUCTIVE DAY." He checked his internal clock—forty-five seconds had passed. Perfect! What efficiency!

"Now, hold on just a minute," Joe said, standing up. "What do you mean, my productivity's negative? What do you mean, 'improvement'?"

Rivet hesitated. He hadn't anticipated this. "DEFINITION: 'IMPROVEMENT': A CHANGE OR ADDITION THAT—"

"I know *that*," Joe interrupted, growing increasingly impatient. "But what do you mean? What are you saying I'm doing wrong? What am I supposed to do differently? I'm working my butt off trying to keep up with the new schedule, you know!"

Rivet searched through his help files, looking for the answers to these questions. "ERM…SEARCHING, PLEASE WAIT," he managed. These questions didn't make sense. Rivet had identified the problem right away and presented it in the most efficient manner. What wasn't this person understanding? "ERROR. BAD COMMAND OR FILE NAME. RETRY? Y/N."

"I…" Joe gritted his teeth. He took a deep breath and fixed a glare on the robot. "Whatever." Turning on his heel, he stormed out of the office, not bothering to close the door.

"HAVE A PRODUCTIVE DAY," Rivet beeped. He did not understand. He recalled situational data from his past experience. Back on the production line, this was the standard way the robots would efficiently handle whatever came up: they always reviewed the facts and addressed the problem head on. None of them ever complained or asked questions; they just carried out the recommended solution.

Rivet did not understand why the humans handled their problems the way they did or even how they managed to solve them at all. Why had his meeting with Joe ended the way it did? What had gone wrong?

"FURTHER ANALYSIS REQUIRED," Rivet chirped to himself. Clearly, there was more to this problem than he'd imagined. He decided he needed to find schematics to study or perhaps find an instruction manual to download.

Troubleshooting

Rivet may have had brand-new titanium-coated parts and the latest updates in polymorphic software, but as any strategic video gamer will tell you, for some tasks a computer just can't match up to a human. Rivet was intimately familiar with machines and their ways, but if you put him in a simple conversation with a person, it would turn one-sided in a hurry, with Rivet on the losing end. Hands down, he was the best chess player in the whole company, but when it was time for charades at the office party celebrating his promotion, Rivet was hopelessly lost.

The biggest issue was that Rivet had spent his whole working life perpetually solving concrete problems with concrete solutions. But his built-in problem-solving methods failed him in his management role. (Imagine that someone promoted to a position requiring skills the person had not yet developed!)

Yet today Rivet is a successful business-bot, a popular and well-respected boss, and a strong leader. With his built-in determination to reach his dream and his natural ability to solve problems, Rivet was able to go far. But one additional asset proved most advantageous: his willingness to learn something new.

Just like you, Rivet was fortunate enough to discover the secrets in this book: a new approach to problem solving that made all the difference in his finally reaching his goals. Certainly, his hard work and determination were important factors, but what really sealed the deal was his introduction to the **step-by-step coaching model** that is outlined, detailed, and illustrated in this book. Rivet's new job challenged him to solve human problems with a human perspective, which he lacked. Following this model, he overcame his troubles—and so can you!

Not only will learning and applying this coaching model help you more efficiently and effectively solve problems in your business (and in your life). Practicing this approach can also lead to what some successful managers call "being a problem-free zone," and it can drastically reduce the amount of precious time that management or employees must spend on problem solving.

Can you imagine your business being a problem-free zone? What could you do with all the newfound time you have had to spend on problem solving? Wherever you are today, that starting place is perfect. Follow Rivet and this step-by-step guide, and you'll learn to use a new tool that you'll find indispensable for your success toolbox. Let's get started!

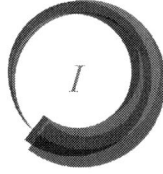

I

AN INTRODUCTION TO COACHING

What Is Coaching?

Chances are, you already have a mental image about what coaching entails, perhaps in a sports-related context. But you may be wondering how this image can be applied to your business to achieve success. Beyond the clear connection between a team sport and a team-driven business, the practice of coaching has much to offer today's small-business owner.

Start with the most basic of basics: What does it mean to be a coach, or to perform the act of coaching?

Because the term *coaching* is itself not unfamiliar, the meaning of coaching in the context of a business environment needs to be clarified, and the key traits of coaching versus other strategies need to be emphasized. Rather than only suggesting that coaching is an effective communication skill, this book is going to give you a full understanding of high-performance coaching, the steps to successfully utilize coaching, and a proven model that you can use as a visual aid to quickly solve any problem through coaching.

This communication will often take place between different individuals, as you might expect, but it can also be an internal process. Self-coaching can sometimes lead to the most significant results of all!

Of course, every situation is different, and one person's preferred (and most effective) interpretation of coaching could vary from the next person's preference. So let's step back a bit and identify coaching by its key traits. What qualities are common to any good coaching strategy, and what would be counterproductive? Let's take a look.

WHAT COACHING IS AND IS NOT!

➤ Coaching has roots in behavioral science (psychology), athletics, and corporate training.

➤ Coaching focuses on the present and helps people move forward toward the future.

COACHING IS

➤ Action oriented
➤ Focused on the future
➤ Goal oriented
➤ Dedicated to growth and success
➤ About asking questions

COACHING IS NOT

➤ Giving advice
➤ Counseling
➤ Fixing people
➤ Doing it for them
➤ Policing

There are many ways to interpret what coaching means for you, but some ways will be more productive than others. When you visualize coaching in the business sphere, here are some images to strive for as well as a few to avoid.

WHAT COACHING IS NOT

- **GIVING ADVICE OR COUNSELING.** Certainly, coaching will call upon you to take plenty of responsibility and initiative, but don't think of it as a one-way street. An advice giver has the answers and assumes the advice recipient does not. This vision of coaching encourages all involved parties to learn from one another and work back and forth toward a universal solution.

- **FIXING PEOPLE, DOING IT FOR THEM, OR POLICING.** A few famous coaches are pretty rough around the edges, but they apparently do get the job done. College basketball coach, Bobby Knight, didn't exactly have the most pleasant demeanor, but Indiana sure did win a lot with him at the helm. So you've got to be rough and tough on people to get results? Not so! In this book, coaching is considered to be a team process, built on a foundation of respect and transparency. A coach takes responsibility for engaging another person in problem solving, but not because that person is helpless or unable to work without the coach. The excellent coach is a catalyst, never a bully.

**Aggressive "communication" may be good for basketball, but not so much for business.
Image via Flickr, by Benji Panic.**

WHAT COACHING IS

- **ACTION ORIENTED.** Initially, coaching is all about communication, but the ultimate point of that communication is to inspire actions that produce results. Coaching is about understanding how things currently are, determining how you want to change things or move things forward, and then *working to make that change happen.*

- **FOCUSED ON THE FUTURE.** As a coach, you should always face forward. Learn from the past, but do not drive forward while looking in the rearview mirror. Be aware of your present situation, but don't become bogged down in it—keep moving toward the future scenario you desire.

- **GOAL ORIENTED.** As the saying goes, Rome was not built in a day. You shouldn't expect success to come right away, nor should you rush forward without having a clear destination in mind. Setting a series of reasonable, attainable goals will keep you going at a steady, satisfying pace, and help you work your way toward ideal outcomes.

- **ABOUT ASKING QUESTIONS.** Fundamentally, coaching begins with inquiry. Just as you cannot map out a route to a desired destination without first knowing where you are now, you must start by asking key questions, engaging yourself and others.

- **DEDICATED TO GROWTH AND SUCCESS.** This image is saved for last, because it's probably the most important. Attitude has everything to do with results. A coach must be *intentionally optimistic* about the success of the team and must foster that attitude at every opportunity. Everyone is naturally resistant to change, and only a positive "let's learn together" attitude will work to move through resistance and on to real improvements.

If this feels like a lot to take in at once, don't worry—the coaching model follows a step-by-step process and you'll be guided through it every step of the way.

A Step-by-Step Guide to Coaching

One reason this model has been proven to work in business environments, no matter the industry or size, is that the process can be understood as six simple steps, each of which comes with its own set of questions:

1. Identify your *topic*: What is the problem, or what do you want to improve?

2. Examine the *current reality*: What's working, and what isn't?

3. Imagine your *vision*: What does your ideal scenario look like?

4. Define *success*: How will you know when you've achieved a desired result, and what can you use to make it happen?

5. Design a plan of *action* (using available *resources*): What will you do to achieve success, with whom, and when?

6. Prepare for *obstacles*: What could get in the way, and how will you overcome it?

The above questions are thought starters. Each of these six steps is covered in depth in subsequent chapters.

Using the coaching model illustrated below will allow you to make a paradigm shift from "fix it" to building on the strengths of an individual and a team to solve their own problems and achieve the desired results to move your business forward.

COACHING MODEL

Steps ▮▮▮▶ **Behaviors** ▮▮▶ **Effects** ▮▮▶ **Results**

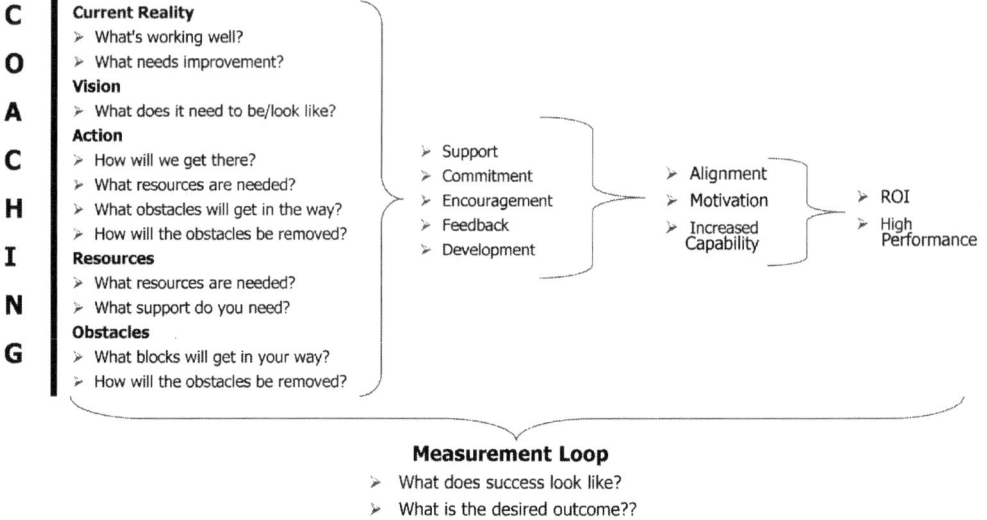

C
O
A
C
H
I
N
G

Current Reality
➤ What's working well?
➤ What needs improvement?

Vision
➤ What does it need to be/look like?

Action
➤ How will we get there?
➤ What resources are needed?
➤ What obstacles will get in the way?
➤ How will the obstacles be removed?

Resources
➤ What resources are needed?
➤ What support do you need?

Obstacles
➤ What blocks will get in your way?
➤ How will the obstacles be removed?

➤ Support
➤ Commitment
➤ Encouragement
➤ Feedback
➤ Development

➤ Alignment
➤ Motivation
➤ Increased Capability

➤ ROI
➤ High Performance

Measurement Loop
➤ What does success look like?
➤ What is the desired outcome??

Aim for Success!

As you walk through each of the six steps, feel free to follow along with the custom-made coaching worksheet (seen in the following section). Or if you prefer, give it a try on your own after reading about all the steps. Along the way, Rivet the Robot will help fill in the blanks.

COACHING MODEL ACTION PLANNING TEMPLATE

TOPIC	What are you going to be working on? What problem do you need to solve?		

CURRENT REALITY	What is working well?	What needs improvement?

VISION	What does it need to be / look like when complete?

SUCCESS	What does success look like? How will you know you achieved the result you want?

ACTION	What are you going to do?	With whom?	By When?

OBSTACLES	What could get in your way?	How will you overcome the obstacle?

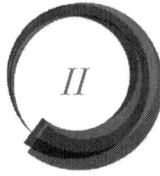

II

COACHING BEHAVIORS AND SKILLS

Recommended Software Update

Frustrated, Rivet barricaded himself in his office, determined to grapple with his problem until he found the proper solution. He found no help in his internal vast database of help files. Interfacing with the computer on his desk, he browsed the Internet, searching for just the right combination of keywords that would draw out the answer he sought. "Robots in management." "Communication between robots and humans." "Business-bots." Unfortunately, none of these seemed to lead to anything relevant to his situation. He tried something more generic: "How to succeed in business."

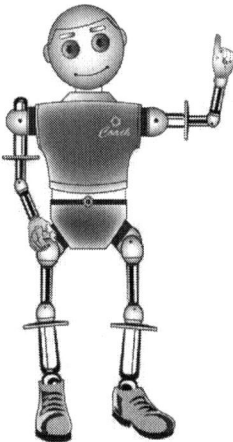

From the pages and pages of results, one word in bold type leaped out at Rivet: **coaching**.

He scanned through his internal files, finding no matches. Here was something he hadn't tried before!

"SUBJECT: COACHING," Rivet beeped aloud. "FURTHER ANALYSIS REQUIRED. DOWNLOADING FILES..."

The Right Tools for the Job

At this point, you're just about ready to begin planning out your long-term coaching strategy. Before you delve into that process, though, it's important to go over some of the basic behaviors and skills you'll need to exhibit and practice in order to succeed in your coaching plan. The reason there's a full chapter covering these concepts in advance is that these qualities will be a fundamental part of the whole coaching process, every step of the way. Practice these behaviors and skills well, as they'll prove instrumental in resolving problems, moving your business forward, and achieving your desired results.

Support

While the principles being covered here can certainly apply to a solo scenario (perhaps involving introspective question-and-answer sessions), the main focus will be on coaching as a one-on-one activity—though it can also work very well if applied to a team. No matter how many people are involved, coaching aims to bring out the best in everyone for the purpose of achieving both personal and company goals.

As a coach, be prepared to analyze your own capabilities as well as those of your teammates, and ask yourself what kind of input you can provide. If a teammate is struggling, don't hesitate to support that person in any way you can—acknowledging any shortfalls and working together to overcome them is one of the keys to high-performance coaching. The fact is that you're all in this together, so the most productive attitude is "We're all in this together!"

Commitment

Coaching doesn't have to be a difficult process, but it does take time, consistency, and persistence. It's very good to be optimistic about growth and the general future, but keep in mind that achieving your goals will take patience and commitment.

When you create your long-term coaching plan, be prepared to commit to it. Most of the results will take time to become visible, and you'll need to be prepared to measure success along the way. If a new idea hasn't yet produced the results you want, try giving it a little more time to develop. Of course, some ideas may simply not pan out. If an idea has had time to work, yet still hasn't bloomed like you'd hoped, you may need to try a different approach—your strongest commitment, after all, should be to the ultimate goal you're after. Continuously moving forward is the key.

Engagement

Basically, practicing good engagement means understanding your own abilities and role within the coaching plan and applying yourself fully to carry it out. Though this behavior focuses on the individual level, it has an important effect on your team dynamic. Ideally, you want your own actions to serve as a model for your fellow team members. By staying positive, motivated, and engaged, you can inspire your team to follow your example. Once everyone has committed to full engagement, success won't be far off!

Development

As the above behaviors have indicated, coaching has a lot to do with identifying your *strengths*, as well as those of your company, and using those strengths effectively. However, understanding your *weaknesses* is just as valuable. Don't think of these aspects only as negative qualities, or as problems that hold you back; consider them more like areas with a higher potential for improvement, or obstacles to be carefully navigated around. In many cases a weakness is simply a "missing part," and identifying and providing it, like adding the fourth tire to a car, can make quite a difference in performance! Naturally, facing forward and focusing on development, or accentuating your strengths and improving in other respects, is a direct means of improving your business on the whole.

Feedback

Make no mistake about it: All of the behaviors presented so far will be very useful to your coaching efforts. That said, if you needed to settle on just one quality as most important, you'd have to zoom in on all things related to feedback. Being able to properly give, receive, and make use of feedback is the surest indicator of a strong, forward-thinking team dynamic.

What makes feedback so crucial to coaching and business growth? That's a pretty big subject, so let's break it up and tackle the basic questions, one at a time.

What Is Feedback?

In brief, *feedback* is what gets communicated back to a person (or a machine!) after an action or a result has occurred. Feedback always occurs (as in "For every action there is an equal and opposite reaction"), but unfortunately it is often ignored. Bringing feedback to the forefront is one of the most direct means of interpersonal problem solving. Basically, it involves one person commenting on the effort of another, pointing out strengths and weaknesses. When all sides involved do their part responsibly and transparently, the feedback process is the best tried-and-true method of finding areas in need of improvement, as well as providing encouragement and praise.

Feedback does involve a major emphasis on highlighting needs for improvement, since it's a very effective method for finding such things, and companies thrive on their ability to improve. However, feedback is not the same as criticism, nor should it be used as such. In the recent analogy about cars and tires, your mechanic should not chastise you for having a flat tire; instead, you need feedback that you need a new tire. When you purchase that fourth tire and your "partner" in problem solving puts it on the car, you're appreciative and ready to roll. People don't like to be told they're doing something wrong—but if you show up as a partner in problem solving, you can be as direct as you want without coming across as negative, harsh, or too demanding. That is exactly what you will be able to do, every time there is a problem, once you learn and practice how to give feedback using this book's model of coaching.

Why Give Feedback?

Feedback does the following:

- **RECOGNIZES AND REWARDS EFFORT.** If people have been performing well, giving them recognition will create a major incentive to keep up the good work. Furthermore, you can say specifically what you liked or what was working well, so as to fine-tune their performance even further.

- **IMPROVES QUALITY.** Regular, honest feedback will keep people's performance improving at a steady rate and prevent them from forming bad habits or falling into a pattern.

- **BUILDS AND MAINTAINS RELATIONSHIPS.** Feedback is a fundamental form of open, honest dialogue, which is essential to a constructive working relationship. Building an environment where feedback can be given openly will create a positive working climate, naturally inspiring trust and support among your team members.

- **CLARIFIES EXPECTATIONS.** When people have a job to do, more often than not they'll prefer to know exactly what to do and how to do it. Giving reliable feedback will create that understanding in your teammates, eliminating any potential guesswork or gray areas. The more open you are about your expectations, the more likely others are to be able to meet them.

How Do I Give Feedback?

There are many ways to approach this topic, but here are some important tips:

- **BE HONEST AND OPEN ABOUT YOUR EXPECTATIONS.** Also, be very clear about how they are, or are not, being met. The less ambiguity you leave in this area, the more likely it is that the person receiving the feedback will benefit from it.

- **FOCUS ON MUTUAL COMMITMENT.** Instead of applying a strict leader-follower dynamic, emphasize the need to work together on an issue. This will communicate your level of involvement and willingness to support your team. Don't simply point out another worker's flaws and instruct that person to fix them; similarly, don't be afraid to receive and utilize feedback yourself.

- **ACKNOWLEDGE POSITIVE PERFORMANCE.** Do this even if (perhaps especially if) your intended focus is to point out room for improvement. Only a lazy manager cannot find something to note that is moving in the right direction, even if the desired result has not yet been fully attained. You want your teammates to look forward to receiving feedback and be motivated enough to use that feedback well—both of which are more likely to happen if you pay attention to positives. In addition, highlighting positives will make any constructive feedback significantly easier both to give and to receive.

- **FRAME THE PROCESS AS ONGOING.** Just like the growth of your company, the growth of an individual is a long-term process that will encompass many, many feedback sessions. Be realistic in your expectations, and make it clear that you're fully invested in the person's ongoing improvement.

Feedback should be tailored to your specific situation, so the shape it takes will be quite unique to your circumstances. That said, you can always start with the foundation of a particular model. For starters, using personal *I* language goes a long way. Examine the chart below:

HOW TO GIVE
CONSTRUCTIVE FEEDBACK

"I" LANGUAGE	EXAMPLE
"When you…	"When you are late to team meetings,
"I feel…	"I get irritated…
"Because I…	"Because I think it is wasting the time of all the other team members, and we are never able to get through all the agenda items."
Pause for Discussion	
"I would like…	"I would like you to consider finding some way of planning your schedule that lets you get to these team meetings on time.
"Because…	"Because that way we can be more productive at the team meetings and we can all keep to our tight schedules."

On the left side of this chart are steps for framing your feedback, or good sentence starters; on the right side are examples of their practical use. Feel free to experiment a bit as you grow more comfortable with the process. But in your early efforts, aim to hit all of these talking points in the right order, and you'll be in great shape.

Giving constructive, difference-making feedback can be a delicate process, and mastering the art will take some time. Still, if you aim to succeed in business—and in general interpersonal interaction, for that matter—you'll need to put in the time and effort to make it a regular part of your routine.

There are many skills and behaviors that will prove important in your quest for business growth. It may seem like a lot to absorb, but it's important to work on these new behaviors one step at a time and not let yourself get overwhelmed. This coaching process is designed to naturally leverage your own strengths, develop these skills, and bring them out in you. Following the steps is as much about personal growth as it is about business success. Jump in, and aim for the top!

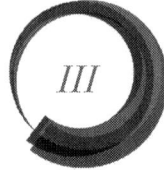

III

IDENTIFYING YOUR TOPIC

Man versus Machine

The software updates were fully installed, but Rivet was still having some trouble getting used to the new speech synthesizer.

"TESTING," he boomed. "OOPS, I SET THE VOLUME TOO HIGH."

He fiddled with a couple of the knobs on his chest control panel.

"TESTING," he said. "Much better! Still feels really weird, though. Now, let's see—where do I start again?"

He searched through all the new files he'd downloaded about **COACHING**. He found his answer, as expected, right near the beginning.

"Ah, that's right," he said. "Figuring out the **topic**!"

The Topic at Hand

This step is a short one, but it's super important! Your topic may be big or small, but either way, it will determine the direction you'll take for every step to come.

Your first task is to sit down and start brainstorming. What, more than anything, is the main problem you're trying to solve? Try to keep the description of the problem as simple as possible—you should be able to sum it up in a single sentence, or better yet, a phrase. For this particular step, it will also help to be more broad than specific.

It will perhaps be easiest if you think of your topic as being synonymous with your goal. For example, you might be interested in using coaching to attract new customers to your business. That's perfectly fine. Your topic could then be "Attracting new customers," or it could be something closely related, such as "Improving visibility in our market."

Though, as previously mentioned, your topic will stick with you for some time, it isn't necessarily set in stone. There are several reasons why you might be inclined to change the topic in the future: Circumstances could change in a way you hadn't expected; your efforts might uncover a previously unseen issue that seems more pressing; or, best-case scenario, your plan could succeed and allow you to reach your goal or solve the problem. In cases like these, it certainly makes sense to go back and start the process again with a fresh topic. Just don't be too quick to do this without a good reason! At the very least, consider sticking with your original topic until you've finished filling out the coaching worksheet.

People, Process, and Safety

Our coaching approach is meant to be extremely flexible, potentially focusing on all sorts of topics. Thus, an experienced user can, with just a few small changes, adapt the model to any situation. To the first-timer, though, this freedom can actually become a creative roadblock right away. If you can use practically anything for your topic, how can you narrow it down to just one distinct concept at a time?

Anytime you're attempting to organize and clarify something, it can be particularly helpful to think in terms of categories. Approaching a problem by first organizing it into a defined group will keep you clear and focused on what sort of issue you're working. Problems found in one manufacturing company are usually very similar to ones found in other plants. Many coaching-appropriate concerns can be neatly sorted into three major categories: **people**, **process**, and **safety**. Of course, as emphasized above, coaching can apply to many more situations; the advanced user is encouraged to branch out and experiment, but it is recommended that new users focus on the following model:

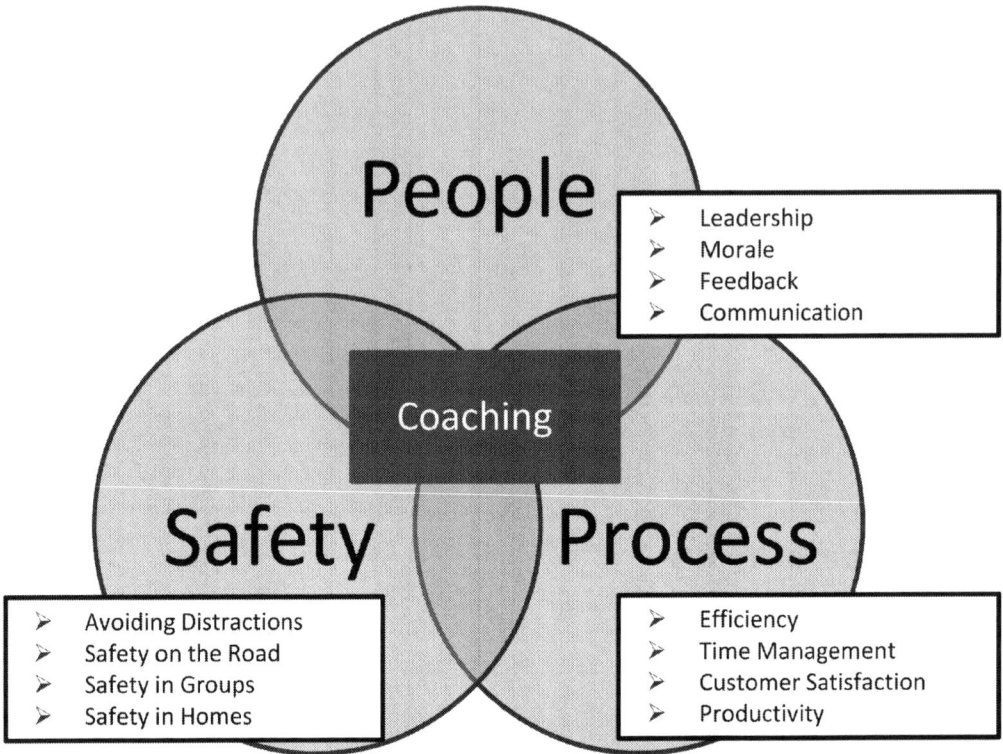

People, process, and safety are ideal concepts for the coaching model.
The boxes contain examples of specific topic ideas.

If you're having trouble narrowing your ideas into one topic, try starting with one of these categories, and think of a few concepts that fit in those guidelines. Consider some of these examples as thought starters:

PEOPLE: COMMUNICATION AND INTERPERSONAL INTERACTION

- Improving relationships with a supervisor, coworker, or employee.

- Becoming a better listener.

- Speaking more effectively in team meetings and group settings.

- Understanding and working through cultural differences.

- Being seen as a team player, and inspiring the same in others.

PROCESS: WORKPLACE PRODUCTIVITY, EFFICIENCY, AND EFFECTIVENESS

- Project management.

- Data-driven planning and measuring results.

- Reducing wasteful activities or behaviors.

- Meeting customer needs better.

- Improving turnaround time on projects or production.

SAFETY: MAINTAINING A POSITIVE, HEALTHY WORK ENVIRONMENT

- Planned inspections and responsibilities.

- Incident investigation.

- Safety guidelines and emergency procedures.

- Performance feedback.

- Hazard recognition and risk assessment.

Any one of these would make an excellent topic for a worksheet and coaching session. If you're stuck, imagine you had to deal with one of the above issues, and think about how you would go through the worksheet with that issue in mind. You can also follow along with Rivet's progress as he fills out the worksheet throughout this book; observing his train of thought and exactly how he works through the steps will provide a sequential model from which you can learn the entire process.

Man versus Machine—Continued

Rivet brainstormed about his **topic** for some time but found himself stuck.

"This coaching thing sure is hard," he sighed. "If only I had some help. Wait, wasn't there something like that in the folder?"

He browsed through his recently downloaded files, and he spotted a program he'd previously overlooked: *Virtual Coach*. Intrigued, he booted it up. After a few moments, a box popped up, prompting him for his name. He typed in "Rivet the Robot," and checked a box to enable "speech mode."

"Good evening, Rivet the Robot," a polite, computerized voice chirped. "What will we be working on today?"

"Well, I'm interested in using this coaching thing to make things better at work," Rivet said. It felt awkward to be conversing with a fellow machine in verbal human language, but he reminded himself it was something he'd need to get used to sooner or later.

"Wonderful," the voice said. "Let us begin with your **topic**. What do you most want to accomplish?"

"That's the tough part," Rivet said. "I feel like there's tons of stuff I need to accomplish. I'm just not sure where to begin!"

"Take your time," the program chirped. "Let us address your concerns one at a time. How would you describe your primary goal in the broadest sense?"

Rivet took a moment to process this. Well, that would certainly make things easier. He tried to decide which of his troubles deserved the most attention. Fundamentally, his woes seemed to all stem from the gap between his robot self and the humans who worked for him.

"I don't know," Rivet said. "I mean, I've got an idea, but it seems too big, too broad. I have no idea how I'd begin to solve it."

"Don't engage your worry button, Rivet the Robot," said Virtual Coach. "Right now, big and broad is exactly what you want! Remember, you'll have plenty of time to figure out how to solve it during the other steps."

"Where should I start, though?" Rivet asked.

"Well, let's try categorizing the issues," the coach said. "Try to think of an issue that's most prominent in your mind right now. Does it have to do with **people**, a **process**, or **safety**?"

Rivet took a moment to think about it. People. Process. Safety...He reflected back on the morning's events and, wincing, thought about the awkward encounter he'd had with Joe Brown.

"People," he said.

"All right," the coach continued. "Let's work from there. What caused the issue, or better yet, what do you think you need to work on in order to prevent it from coming up again in the future? If it's a people issue, you might find it helpful to think about communication and your overall team dynamic."

"Hmm, that makes sense," Rivet said. "I think I can work with that."

He turned to the worksheet:

COACHING MODEL ACTION PLANNING TEMPLATE

TOPIC	What are you going to be working on? What problem do you need to solve?
	Better communication with human employees.

CURRENT REALITY	What is working well?	What needs improvement?
	•	•

VISION	What does it need to be / look like when complete?
	•

SUCCESS	What does success look like? How will you know you achieved the result you want?
	•

ACTION	What are you going to do?	With whom?	By When?
	1.	•	•

OBSTACLES	What could get in your way?	How will you overcome the obstacle?
	•	•

IV

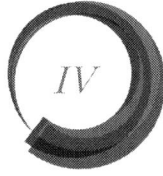

UNDERSTANDING YOUR CURRENT REALITY

The Pros and Cons of Robotics

"Say, that was pretty easy after all," Rivet said. "Thanks, Virtual Coach!"

"Of course," the coaching program said. "Feel free to ask more questions when you need to. I am here to help."

With the Virtual Coach's advice, coming up with an appropriate **topic** had taken Rivet only a few moments of calculation. After all, the problem was staring him in the face every time he shared a room with a human employee; thus far, the man-machine interface just wasn't working out.

Thinking of his situation, Rivet felt frustration and irritation welling up again. Why was management proving to be so difficult? It wasn't fair! He began to wonder if even something as promising as **coaching** could help him improve.

"All right, I need to calm down," he said to himself, cooling down his circuits. "Maybe some music would help." He put on one of his favorite synth-pop tunes, cranked the volume down to an ambient level, and glanced over the next section of the worksheet.

"**Current reality**, huh?" he said. "Let's see, first I should ask what's not working well."

Well, that part was certainly easy! Rivet could think of a million things that weren't going well. The hard part would be narrowing it down to something he could work with!

"Okay, can't let myself get discouraged," he said. "Let's move on to the next one: What *is* working well? Hmm."

He sat back for a moment, running his processors. This would take some thought, he realized. On the bright side, he noticed that the more he used them, the more comfortable he was getting with his new speech synthesizer and thought modules. Maybe now was a prime time to test out the new on-board coffee dispenser as well...

The Here and Now

Before you can properly tackle any problem, big or small, you have to understand what you're dealing with. In our coaching model, this is called "taking stock of your **current reality**."

Start by asking yourself any number of basic questions about the situation. What is the issue at hand? Is it most associated with **people**, with a **process,** or with **safety**? How do you hope to improve? Why are you in the current situation—what obstacles are preventing improvement? Who is actively involved in this process? How do those people feel about the situation? You might know the answers to some of these questions right away, while others could go unanswered for a good while. That's perfectly okay at this stage. Right now, you're just brainstorming to get the fullest possible sense of where you are and what you're facing.

You're free to address whatever questions or concerns you like. If you think exploring something will be helpful, don't hesitate to include it! That said, when you're using the coaching template, you'll probably find it useful to cover these important bases:

- **WHAT ARE YOU GOING TO BE WORKING ON? WRITE ANY QUESTIONS AND ANSWERS IN THE "TOPIC" FIELD.**
  It's a simple step, but it will prove effective at keeping your thoughts focused and your actions on track throughout the process to come. What is the core concern you plan to address using coaching? This can start out as a broad or vague idea ("Profits were down last quarter," for example), but as you brainstorm, see if you can use the information you have to make it more specific ("My business isn't attracting as many new customers as it was last year.") The more focused your topic is, the easier it'll be to come up with an effective solution.

- **WHAT IS WORKING WELL? FILL IN THE LEFT HALF OF "CURRENT REALITY."** Even if you feel like things just aren't going right anywhere, take some time to think about what you and your business are doing well, whether big or small. Not only will this boost your confidence but also will it help point out behaviors and trends that you can emphasize to promote growth and success.

- **WHAT NEEDS IMPROVEMENT? FILL IN THE RIGHT HALF OF "CURRENT REALITY."** Think of realistic goals for the near future, and again, be specific, if possible. At this point, if you can come up with potential solutions, that's great; feel free to include them. At the very least, though, identify what needs to improve, even if you can't yet decide how to do it. Be honest, but avoid criticism or casting blame on individuals. Remember, a major part of being accountable is taking responsibility as a team!

Better Brainstorming Tips
Are you having trouble coming up with those bullet points? Here are a few questions you might try asking to find that spark of inspiration.

- **WHAT IS THE OPPORTUNITY HERE?** What is the something you can currently take advantage of? Where do you have room to grow, or what sets you apart from someone else in your field? Besides using this to help you think of new strengths, you can also ask the question to build from one strength to another, or to build from a strength to an area that's in need of improvement. Okay, your business is really great at this particular task; now how can you use that to emphasize other strengths, or to cover for a weakness elsewhere?

- **WHAT ARE THE DRIVERS?** What do you see as your primary motivator? This in itself can be a strength, or possibly an issue to work on in the future. This is true whether the driver in question is a carrot or a stick, so to speak. A desire for great rewards and satisfaction can be a very powerful motivator, and so can a strong desire to avoid a particular bad outcome, but both can easily lead to undue stress if they're left unchecked.

- **WHAT ARE THE BARRIERS?** If you had to name just one thing, what is preventing you from achieving your goal? Furthermore, what might become a bigger obstruction in the future? As will be covered later on in chapter VIII, "Overcoming Potential Obstacles," no barrier is insurmountable, especially if you anticipate it and come up with a workaround early on.

The Pros and Cons of Robotics, Continued

"I think I need help again, Virtual Coach," Rivet said.

"Current step: **current reality**," Virtual Coach beeped. "Now's the time to brainstorm freely! Just get all of your thoughts on the worksheet— what's working well, and what isn't?"

"I suppose that's easy enough," Rivet said. "How much should I write, though?"

"As much as you want," the coach replied. "The more, the better! I recommend at least trying to balance the 'working well' and 'needs improvement' columns, but besides that, there are no restrictions whatsoever."

"Hmm," Rivet said, sizing up the worksheet. "Still, there's not a whole lot of space to write much, is there?"

"Now, Rivet the Robot, you know that's not true," the coach said. "You're using an electronic document, so you can make the space as big as you need!"

"Oh yeah, you're right," Rivet said, feeling more than a little sheepish. He started putting down bullet points in the boxes, switching back and forth.

COACHING MODEL ACTION PLANNING TEMPLATE

TOPIC	**What are you going to be working on? What problem do you need to solve?** Better communication with human employees.

	What is working well?	**What needs improvement?**
CURRENT REALITY	• Good at problem solving Years of experience on the product floor; familiarity with the business • Unlimited access to organic data via internet • New speech working perfectly! • So is the coffee dispenser!	• Need to understand how best to speak to employees • What motivates them/makes humans comfortable • Social environment is strained, tense

	What does it need to be / look like when complete?
VISION	•

	What does success look like? How will you know you achieved the result you want?
SUCCESS	•

	What are you going to do?	**With whom?**	**By When?**
ACTION	1.	•	•

	What could get in your way?	**How will you overcome the obstacle?**
OBSTACLES	•	•

V

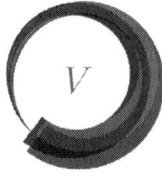

CREATING YOUR VISION

A Bright Future for Robotkind

Rivet finished typing, and glanced over his work so far. Already a third of the way done? Remarkable! This gave him a new sense of confidence—success was that much closer and within his reach.

"We make a great team, don't we, Virtual Coach?" Rivet said.

"We sure do, Rivet the Robot," the coach said. "I'll be here when you need me!"

Perhaps it was just a glitch in Rivet's sensory suite, but he could almost feel bits and bytes of satisfaction and validation. Really taking the time to analyze his strengths as well as his shortfalls had been beneficial, as well. He reviewed his less-than-satisfactory initial attempts at humor and noted that the new JokeTeller program was an excellent addition to his setup. Though they'd been hard to understand at first, he now especially appreciated the "comic relief" features. He considered going back and adding that to the "working well" section, but JokeTeller's Humor Wizard advised him not to push his luck.

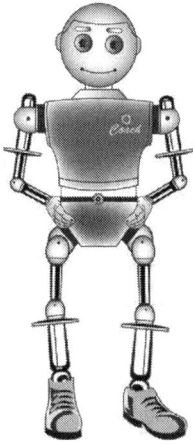

"Well, at this rate, I'll be respected far and wide in no time," Rivet said. "Man, that'll be the day. I'll be such an effective communicator I'll just be riveting*!" he joked to himself.*

The thought was intoxicating, even to a nuts-and-bolts machine like Rivet. Firing up a graphic-design program, he allowed himself to get lost in drawing an optimistic picture of his future self. He drew himself towering over Joe Brown and his other human teammates, a giant, platinum-plated beacon of empowerment for all robotkind.

"Wait, no," he said. "Maybe that sends an entirely wrong message."

He undid the last few steps and made some key adjustments. First he lessened the height disparity between his avatar and the human figures (it had been pretty self-serving anyway, he realized). He didn't want to simply lead the humans, or wield power over them (despite what any number of sci-fi films depict in no uncertain terms). Rivet wanted to be respected as an equal and be allowed to hold a position of responsibility because of communication competence, not just lightning-fast mathematics or assembly-line precision. Thinking positive robot-thoughts, he sketched a crowd of applauding, cheering teammates and linked them, both humans and robots. He even put good old Joe Brown, now the happiest human of all, up on his own big, boxy shoulders.

Rivet admired his work, his emotional circuits running a full-pride algorithm. Then he noticed the task bar, and he felt the pride start to reset to *dread* as he saw first the tab for his neglected worksheet, then the clock display.

"Geez, how did that take up so much time?" Rivet grumbled. "It wasn't even that good a drawing!"

"Well, no sense grousing about it now," he added. He pulled the worksheet back up and looked at the next empty box: "**vision**: What does it need to be/look like?"

"*Look* like, huh?" Rivet mused, glancing back at his drawing. "How very convenient!" A picture, according to his Idiom Generator (recently updated with a Cliché 2.0 add-on), was worth a thousand words. All he had to do, it seemed, was pick the ones that mattered the most!

An Optimistic Vision

Our next step involves constructing a **vision** of your ideal coaching outcome. Of course, you don't have to literally draw a picture like Rivet did. But if it helps, by all means, don't hold back!

Whatever medium you choose to use, your goal at this stage is to get a sense of your finish line. Having filled in your **topic** and **current reality**, you should already have a fairly good idea of your ultimate goal.

What distinguishes this step from the others, though, is the required level of focus. During the **topic** stage, you were encouraged to come up with something broader or more general. Now it's time to delve into specifics. Picture your ideal end result—such as a 20 percent more profitable business, or a healthier social atmosphere in the workplace—and zoom in on the details. What, specifically, makes your business profitable, and what kinds of little practices and tweaks keep it that way? How do employee interactions play out now that any tension has been dispelled, and what role do you play in all of it? It's okay to imagine a truly ideal outcome, even if it feels like you are shooting for the moon. Remember, this step is about defining the ideal and painting a clear picture, like filling in the smooth area where you want to land between the craters on your moon.

These are some intensely engaging questions, to be sure, and they won't necessarily be easy to answer. Fortunately, by following along up to this point, you have the tools you need to get started. If you're having trouble with defining the details, go back to **current reality** and reflect on what you wrote there. Think about the individual points on the "working well" side. How can you emphasize or encourage that strength and/or expand its presence? What will the visible result be once you've done that? Also zoom in on the points you filled in on the "needs improvement" side, one at a time. What measures could you take to alleviate that particular issue, and what would your overall business procedure look like if those measures became permanent?

The overall coaching process involves quite a bit of big-picture thinking throughout, but now is definitely the time to start thinking about it as a forward-moving process. If you take a cue from Rivet's creative side and give the visioning process a distinct shape, it would look like the following:

VISIONING

			CURRENT REALITY	VISION
			Find common ground	**Find a desired future**
H I N D S I G H T	L E A R N I N G	A N A L Y Z E	What is the opportunity here?	What is here that we can explore?
			Where might we improve?	What is one more possibility?
			How does if fit with the plans?	What are some other options?
			What do you think that means?	What can we do to be more effective?
			What is your assessment?	How can we add more value?

PAST   **PRESENT**   *FUTURE FORESIGHT*   *FUTURE*

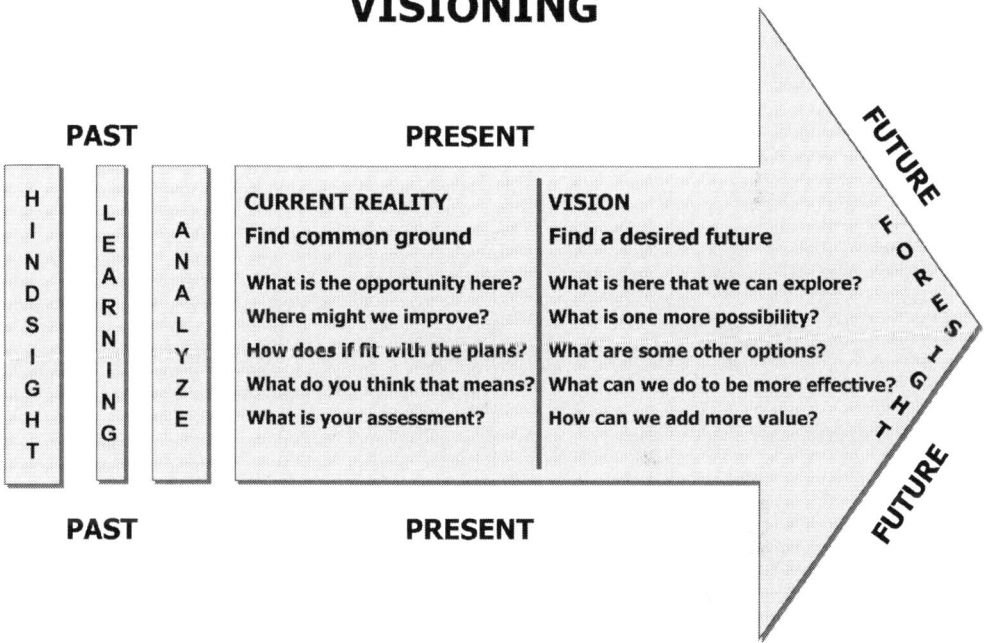

Visioning is an exploration through time, from past to present to future.

Essentially, by following the process in order, you've been carrying out a natural progression through time, just like in the chart above. You start with the past, examine the present, and ultimately arrive at the future. Whatever the issues or concerns that led you to try out this coaching model, they were products of your business's past and present, and analyzing your **current reality** encouraged you to take stock of these phases. In a nutshell, you asked this question: Where are you now (present), and what led you to this point (past)? When you determined your **topic**, you caught a brief glimpse of the future. Now, starting with **vision**, from here on out you'll need to keep most of your focus on the future. Of course, you'll want to look at the present as well, since you'll need to draw upon your business's current resources. But the aim will be to build a better future.

Better Brainstorming Tips

If you're in danger of feeling overwhelmed by all this abstract brainstorming, never fear! To uncloud your crystal ball, try asking a few of these questions:

- **WHAT CAN YOU EXPLORE?** At this stage in the brainstorming process, try not to be too concerned about limiting your thought process or grounding yourself in any set expectations. Some of the best ideas may seem, at first, farfetched. Mentally follow it into your future **vision** and see where it might take you. If you can imagine it, you can do it!

- **WHAT IS ONE MORE POSSIBILITY?** Don't feel compelled to restrict yourself to just one **vision**. The future is, by its very nature, unpredictable, and any number of factors could contribute to all sorts of different outcomes. Imagine a different result—it could be better, worse, or simply different—and make preparations for that result, too. If things happen to lead to that outcome instead, you won't be caught off guard, and in any case, you'll have a good backup plan.

- **HOW CAN YOU ADD MORE VALUE?** While Rivet's story is meant to emphasize the value of coaching as a one-on-one process, don't hesitate to bring in your teammates and encourage them to contribute. What are their **visions**, and how are these similar or different compared to yours? Remember, a coach who listens to the team's players has a much stronger team and a much better chance of reaching the goal!

A Brighter Future for Robotkind, Continued

"I just don't understand modern art." Rivet sighed, turning the drawing over again and again, trying to recall what he'd had in mind when he drew it.

"Come now, Rivet," Virtual Coach beeped. "Clearly, you have a sense of what your ideal **vision** looks like! You just need to find a way to express it in a practical sense."

"But I'm having trouble finding the right words to describe it," Rivet said.

"No one said it needed to be described in words. Even just the picture could be enough, if it makes sense to you," the coach replied. "You just need to ground your **vision** in something concrete that you can accurately describe. More specificity is better, as it will make it all the easier to recognize when that **vision** becomes **reality**!"

"Ah, that makes sense," Rivet said. "I think I've got it now. I think I will stick to using words, though."

"Do whatever makes the most sense to you," the coach said.

Glancing back and forth between the picture and the worksheet, Rivet brainstormed ways to describe it:

COACHING MODEL ACTION PLANNING TEMPLATE

TOPIC	What are you going to be working on? What problem do you need to solve?
	Better communication with human employees.

CURRENT REALITY	What is working well?	What needs improvement?
	• Good at problem solving Years of experience on the product floor; familiarity with the business • Unlimited access to organic data via internet • New speech working perfectly! • So is the coffee dispenser!	• Need to understand how best to speak to employees • What motivates them/makes humans comfortable • Social environment is strained, tense

VISION	What does it need to be / look like when complete?
	• I want to maintain my business owner's responsibility • My human teammates respect me (maybe because we understand how we're similar?) • We are friendly with each other (I help them out, and they help me!) • I have credibility as a professional

SUCCESS	What does success look like? How will you know you achieved the result you want?
	•

ACTION	What are you going to do?	With whom?	By When?
	1.	•	•

OBSTACLES	What could get in your way?	How will you overcome the obstacle?
	•	•

VI

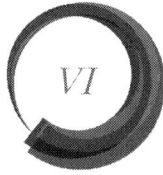

ACHIEVING SUCCESS

One Giant Leap for Robotkind

Rivet's **vision** was optimistic, to be sure, but then right from the beginning, this robot showed he was a dreamer. Even if he wasn't fully aware of it himself, it was one of his strongest traits! Certainly, it was helping him picture the future he wanted as well as giving him the personal drive to work toward it.

"Halfway there already!" Rivet said. "Sorry to keep you up so late, Virtual Coach."

"Don't worry, Rivet the Robot," the coach said. "I'm a very leading-edge computer program, and I don't require much downtime at all. You should take a break every now and then, though!"

Rivet had to admit that it seemed like an attractive proposal. He checked the clock. It had gotten very late, and Rivet had been the only worker at the company for hours, except for the night-shift security guard, Georgia Wilson. As if on cue, she passed by Rivet's open door, flashlight in hand. Peering inside, she tensed up and tightened her grip on the flashlight, but she relaxed when she saw the solitary robot calculating away. It was well-known throughout the company that Rivet, as a robot, didn't need to sleep, and Georgia had grown accustomed to seeing the mechanical man cheerfully at work in his office long after closing time.

"You all right in here, Mr. Rivet?" she said, stifling a yawn. "You need anything?"

"No, thank you," Rivet chirped. Hearing the reply, Georgia paused, wearing a puzzled expression.

"You sure you're okay, boss?" she said. "You sound, uh, kinda different."

"Just a software update," he said.

"Ah, gotcha, I think," she replied. "Sounds good! It sounds, uh, very natural."

Rivet's robot features couldn't convey it, but inwardly he felt a surge of happiness. Georgia gave him a half wave and turned to leave.

"Oh, just a moment, Ms. Wilson," Rivet said. "You seem a little tired. Would you like a cup of coffee?"

She beamed, slightly confused, but grateful nonetheless. "Gee, sounds like your update came with mind-reading software, too!" she said. She glanced around the office. "Um, where's the coffee maker?"

"In a moment," Rivet said. He punched in a few commands on his button array and switched on the coffee valve in his chest compartment.

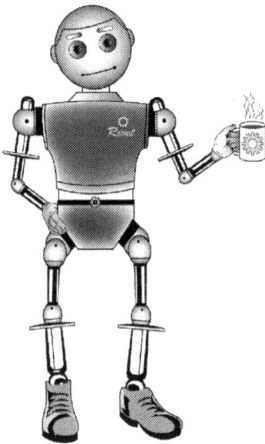

After thirty seconds, he opened a panel and pulled out a paper cup full of piping hot joe. "Here you go!"

"Mr. Rivet, you sure are full of surprises," Georgia said, accepting the gift. "Thanks a bunch!"

"Of course," he said. "And please, just call me Rivet. You and I are on the same team, after all!"

Feeling much perkier, Georgia left the office, whistling an off-key tune.

It hadn't been much, but Rivet still felt like he'd just scored a real achievement. Now that was the kind of interaction he was looking for! If only his talk with Joe Brown had gone half as well, he mused.

If this little exchange was any indication of what he could do on a larger scale, he'd reach his **vision** in no time! Clearly, he had the resources needed to achieve **success**; he just needed to figure out how to maximize their potential. He brewed himself a celebratory cup of coffee of his own and got down to business on the next step.

A *Vision of Success*

Ready to do some time traveling? For this step, maintain your strong focus on the future. As you saw in the previous chapter, this is the chart:

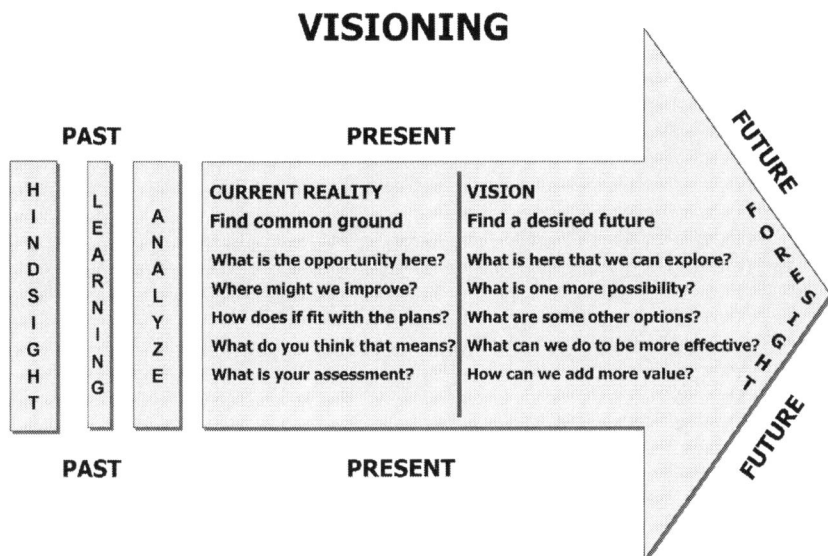

VISIONING

PAST		PRESENT		FUTURE

| H I N D S I G H T | L E A R N I N G | A N A L Y Z E | CURRENT REALITY
Find common ground

What is the opportunity here?
Where might we improve?
How does if fit with the plans?
What do you think that means?
What is your assessment? | VISION
Find a desired future

What is here that we can explore?
What is one more possibility?
What are some other options?
What can we do to be more effective?
How can we add more value? | FORESIGHT |

PAST		PRESENT		FUTURE

First of all, you need to consider the picture of your eventual **success**. How will you know for sure when you've achieved the goal you set up in your **topic**? What specific indicators should you look for? Looking back on your **current reality** will help a great deal here. When you've noticeably cleared up one of the bullet points on the "room for improvement" side, you'll know you're that much closer to your goal. When you've cleared up all of them, chances are it's time to reach for an even higher goal!

This part of the step shares a lot in common with the previous one, **vision**. After you've become comfortable with the coaching process and you begin to use it on a regular basis, you may even prefer to do the two parts simultaneously, as they go hand in hand. Figuring out your **success** involves measurement of the steps to reach your established **vision**.

Of course, it certainly won't hurt to do both steps in quick succession and play them off of one another. Think critically about the future you want to achieve, and above all, stay optimistic. Following the steps to come, you'll be able to make it a reality!

One Giant Leap for Robotkind, Continued

Rivet gulped down the coffee, savoring the odd feeling of the hot beverage circulating his system.

"What about you, Virtual Coach?" Rivet asked. "Would you like a cup of coffee, too?"

"Thank you for the considerate offer, Rivet the Robot," the coach said politely. "Unfortunately, I am a computer program and cannot drink coffee."

"Right, sorry," Rivet said. Only now did making that offer strike him as outlandish—these humanlike behaviors he was practicing were really blurring his existential senses!

"Anyway, how is your progress on the worksheet?" the coach asked. "Ah, I see you're already on the **success** section!"

"Yes, that's true," Rivet said. "It seems kind of strange, though. It says I'm supposed to think about how I will know when I've gotten the right result, but didn't I basically already do that just now?"

"You're right—the two steps are quite similar," the coach said. "What sets them apart is measurement."

"Measurement?" Rivet echoed. "What do you mean?"

"Well, when you did the **vision** step, you were just focusing on one point in the future, speculating about what it would look like," the coach replied. "For this step, though, try to imagine yourself working your way up to that. What will it take to get there, and how will you be able to tell that you're making progress? That's where measurement will come in."

"Hmm," Rivet said. "I think I can see what you mean."

"Take your time, and feel free to ask questions if you're stuck," the coach said. "I'll walk you through it, so don't worry—for now, just put down whatever comes to mind."

"Sure thing," Rivet said. He started typing.

COACHING MODEL ACTION PLANNING TEMPLATE

TOPIC	What are you going to be working on? What problem do you need to solve?
	Better communication with human employees.

CURRENT REALITY	What is working well?	What needs improvement?
	• Good at problem solving Years of experience on the product floor; familiarity with the business • Unlimited access to organic data via internet • New speech working perfectly! • So is the coffee dispenser!	• Need to understand how best to speak to employees • What motivates them/makes humans comfortable • Social environment is strained, tense

VISION	What does it need to be / look like when complete?
	• I want to maintain my business owner's responsibility • My human teammates respect me (maybe because we understand how we're similar?) • We are friendly with each other (I help them out, and they help me!) • I have credibility as a professional

SUCCESS	What does success look like? How will you know you achieved the result you want?
	• When I've achieved my minor goals and feel happy and fulfilled at work • Having intimate knowledge of the business industry • I'm established as an expert • Experience on the assembly line helps me bridge between workers and management • I use my skills to help others, and they feel appreciated, not threatened!

ACTION	What are you going to do?	With whom?	By When?
	1.	•	•

OBSTACLES	What could get in your way?	How will you overcome the obstacle?
	•	•

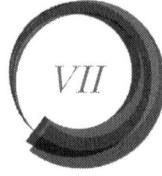

VII

MAKING TIME FOR ACTION

A Robot's Got to Do What a Robot's Got to Do

"So that's how you do the **success** step," the Virtual Coach said. "Does that make sense?"

"Yes, I believe so," Rivet said. "Thanks, Virtual Coach! I don't know how I'd get through any of this without your help."

"Of course, Rivet the Robot," the coach said. "That's what I was programmed for! Feel free to call for me if you have further questions."

At the moment, Rivet's motivation levels were running far higher than his hardware and system specifications claimed to support. Being a machine had its limitations, for sure, but it also came with a whole lot of bonuses, and he realized that all he needed to do was spin those in a way that covered for the downsides. Whirring and clicking, he fired up a couple of calculus graphing apps and found that, after just a bit of brainstorming and busy work, his probability of success over time was quickly approaching infinity!

Now, he just had to come up with a way to make his desired **success** a reality. Fortunately, one of the strengths that came with being a robot involved being able to predict fairly easily the possible outcomes of a mind-boggling array of various actions. He could just treat his problems like a game of chess; and just like his prototype-hood hero, Deep Blue, he could triumph over his own personal Kasparov. Thinking of it, though, he figured he should start to go easier on his break-room chess opponents. From his new perspective, handing out so many crushing defeats to coworkers seemed a bit bad for morale, and it didn't help his chances of being accepted as a teammate. Rivet knew he needed to apply his emotion-sensitization booster, which he was counting on to improve his communication with humans.

"Let's see—now I've got to come up with **actions**," he noted. He thought back on the recent exchange with Georgia, the security guard. "Well, I don't know if I can make things better just by giving everyone coffee…although that's not a bad start."

Deep in meditation, like a grandmaster before a championship game, Rivet began planning out his strategy. First, he had to get his pieces in place; for the most part, his updates and attempts at self-improvement had gotten that rolling. Then he had to use them intelligently. How that would translate to real-life behaviors in the business sphere was still unknown, but as he set about writing, his processors ran at blinding speed to find the answer…

Now's the Time to Take Action—or Plan Them Out, Anyway!

Hopefully, in the midst of all the brainstorming about your business's present and future, you spent some time focusing on how the strengths in your **current reality** could be used to achieve **success**. If so, great! This step will simply expand on all of that, so it will be very easy to get started on. Even if you haven't yet had the chance to think about such topics, though, you'll still be building on the work you've done so far, so you're already well on your way!

This is it: the critical step you've been waiting for. Now is the time for **action**! You won't yet be actually executing any of the plans you write here—that will come a little later, once the worksheet is all filled out— but this step will lead directly to the exciting step of using all of your planning and hard work to score a big payoff. Keep it up! You're doing great so far, and you're almost there!

Think of this section like a road map or perhaps a movie script. Each **action** you plan to take will be set up like a scene or a plot point, and you'll ask yourself some appropriate accompanying questions. First of all, what are you going to do? Second, with whom are you going to do it? Third, when will this take place? Remember, you are the author of your **success** script.

The **action** section will cover the important basics, but if you want to keep going, you may want to give yourself even more details—using extra room, the back of the worksheet, or another piece of paper. For instance, where will you be when you carry this out? Just as an example, say you plan to have a calm, constructive talk with some teammates about showing a negative attitude on the job. Typically, doing it in private would be the most tactful option, but you want to avoid framing it in a way that seems like intimidation or a power play. For example, you could pull the people aside individually in the break-room, instead of summoning them to your office. Another good question: Why will you take this particular step? Chances are, answering this question will involve reviewing what you covered earlier in the worksheet, but it can be a helpful tool for keeping track of how all the little pieces will fall into place as you move forward toward your goal.

At this point, you're free to allow yourself plenty of wiggle room, and you can edit any or all aspects of a task on the fly if a good reason for it comes up. Just be sure that you're happy with it when you finish the worksheet, because sticking to your plans will be important once it's time to actually carry them out! If you like, you can keep a list of your actions in a notebook or another small, separate location and treat it like a to-do list, checking each one off as it's completed, and perhaps even marking items in a different way if they directly led to an achieved goal. Sometimes, little bursts of satisfaction like these are all that you need to keep going forward!

The Resourceful Businessperson

Naturally, the **action** step has a lot to do with *what* you're going to do, but considering *how* you'll accomplish it is also critical. Recall the brief discussion of drawing on the strengths listed in your **current reality**; this section will be fairly similar. To get closer to your goal, take stock of your available **resources**.

What can count as a **resource**? For the purpose of the coaching model, this concept can be defined as literally anything your business has that may specifically help you achieve your goal. Resources can be particular people, places, or things; they can even be more abstract concepts, such as skills, opportunities, or your business's history, brand, and reputation. A **resource's** function may be relatively obvious—say, for example, cash on hand; or it can be more open to interpretation—for instance, time.

Focusing on the present, your next step is to come up with a list of strengths, possessions, and other beneficial traits that your business has *right now* that can be used with **actions** leading to your **success**. Don't sell yourself short—your business is sure to have many solid **resources** that are within your grasp and, regardless of how they're being used now, can be leveraged into major growth and improvement. Often you can find **resources** "hiding in plain sight," once you take time to focus and uncover them. If you struggled earlier to fill in the "What works" section of **current reality**, now's the time to revisit the topic and challenge yourself. Don't move on until you've filled in that whole box!

As you take stock of your current **resources**, you may find it helpful to consider them in relation to the various minor improvements and subgoals you've come up with so far, as opposed to just the big goal in your **topic**. It may be difficult to connect a given strength to the big-picture **success** you've outlined, but if you use it to fix a smaller issue, and that leads you closer to your ideal outcome, that certainly counts for a lot!

The task of uncovering and identifying **resources** has many practical applications, as you'll be able to better appreciate and make use of your **resources** on your way to your goal. But you definitely need to acknowledge the motivational side of it. Remember that even in the gloomiest of circumstances, you can always count on a **resource** to help lift you up! The trick, of course, is looking for and finding it. Just keep looking, bring in teammates for input if you're stuck (or if you're not—either way, they can be very helpful), and don't stop until there are both obvious and newly uncovered **resources** "present and accounted for."

Going for Goals the SMART *Way*
As you're setting up your **action** plans and tying them into the various goals you aim to fulfill, there are a few tips you'll want to keep in mind.

To sum it up in one word, you'll want to be "SMART." Why the all-caps, you ask? Because it's a handy acronym, of course!

SMART = specific, measurable, actionable, relevant, timely.

Chances are you've seen this goal-setting tool before. There's a reason why it has become widespread (and no one knows who made it up first!): because it's brilliantly simple and effective. So what does each of the criteria for setting "smart" goals mean?

- **SPECIFIC.** You may remember the advice from a few chapters back on tying your strengths and resources to smaller, more specific goals, rather than the big, broad one from your **topic**. That's very relevant here, too. Assuming your **topic** is appropriately open-ended, it's unreasonable to expect to be able to take care of it with any single, all-encompassing action. The purpose of this section, and several of the sections that preceded it, is to break that big goal into a number of smaller steps and work your way to success, one manageable piece at a time. You should end up with a variety of **actions** planned out, and each one should focus on contributing to a specific, small subgoal. Example: A too-general goal of "increasing sales" could have, as one of many subgoals, the specific task of producing sixty additional widgets per day.

- **MEASURABLE.** A given **action** may be helpful, but it'll be tough to feel any sense of satisfaction if it's not clear how the action helped you, or if you don't have a way of knowing if the action was even helpful in the first place. Think back to the first part of the **success** phase, when you thought about what particular markers would indicate that you'd achieved your big goal. Get into the habit of asking this question: Will this **action** produce accurate data, and will we be able to identify and/or measure it? Example: What would it take to produce sixty additional widgets? One action could be to speed up the assembly process. To be specific and measurable, you would say, "Move Robot GT-6 to Assembly Line 2 (AL2) for two additional hours each day," since you know Robot GT-6 can add thirty widgets per hour to production.

- **ACTIONABLE.** Interestingly, when you think about it, you cannot actually "manage productivity" or "time," but you can manage **actions**. No result is produced without action(s), and, while simple, it is also crucial in goal setting to think in terms of actions. You will need to create a task that is clear and easy to understand. Also, an "actionable" goal is one that has clearly defined conditions of satisfaction. Example: Assembly Line 2 supervisor must move the GT-6 Robot from the shipping department to AL2 to work from 1:00 p.m. to 3:00 p.m. and then have it returned to shipping. The conditions of satisfaction are these: (1) GT-6 is fully functioning for two hours on AL2; (2) sixty additional widgets are assembled on AL2 each day; and (3) Robot GT-6 is returned, fully functioning, to the shipping department by 3:15 p.m.

- **RELEVANT.** This may seem obvious, but it can be surprisingly easy to get caught up in free-form brainstorming and wind up with a lot of ambitious-sounding plans that, in practice, probably won't address the goals at hand. Stay grounded in your **topic** and your subgoals, and try to stick to **actions** that have a clear connection to them and/or are likely to produce useful results and information. Example: When bringing Robot GT-6 to mind as a resource, you may think of other ways this unit could fill in throughout the plant and be used more effectively. You can make a side note about that, but stay on track in defining actions to achieve your "sixty additional widgets" goal.

- **TIMELY.** A well-planned **action** may be a splendid idea, but it still needs to be executed at the right time to get the best results. When you're planning your timetable and filling in the "When" box, think about how the tasks should be logically ordered, as well as how they might best capitalize on predicted time-sensitive trends or opportunities. More advanced users may even want to plan a series of timed actions as a chain reaction of sorts—one task will produce data that will contribute to the success of a subsequent item, which can in turn lead to the next one, and so on. Example: No matter how planned out your action step is of borrowing Robot GT-6 for AL2, clarifying time parameters is imperative. If GT-6 is in the shop for upgrades until next month, that must be factored in.

Remember to stay SMART, and you'll be well on your way to turning your to-do list into a *can*-do list!

Collaboration with teammates is always a helpful part of the coaching process, but during this step it's especially crucial, since many of your planned **actions** will involve one or more people. If you plan to have a particular teammate actively participate in a task, make sure you include that person in the planning process! It is (unnecessarily) difficult for people to be enthusiastic about a growth objective that's sprung on them without any input or consent. Improvement always means change, and the more involved people are in creating the plan for change, the more they can be counted on to see that the changes are accepted and implemented.

Overall, as you carry out this step, be sure to carefully consider all of the information you've brainstormed about up to this point, and take all the time you need to develop realistic **action** plans. You'll be carrying these plans out and actively engaging with all your SMART goals in the very near future. Stay positive, stay focused, and work your way toward success!

A Robot's Got to Do What a Robot's Got to Do…Continued

"This seems like a really hard part, Virtual Coach," Rivet said. "I mean, this is really the most important step, isn't it? This will decide whether or not the whole thing succeeds down the line!"

"It is indeed important," the coach agreed. "However, try not to get *too* caught up in thinking about the what-ifs. Remember, any idea is potentially worth considering—you just have to be willing to brainstorm it out!"

"Well, all right, I can do that," Rivet said. "How should I get started, though?"

"Just treat it like a to-do list," the coach suggested. "Think about your goals and desires from the previous steps, and think about how you'd go about fulfilling them. Start with the short term, and work your way up to the long term. Once you get started, I think you'll find it much easier to keep going from there."

"That sounds like a good idea," Rivet said. "All right, I'll give it a shot! Let's see what I can come up with."

Rivet took the coach's advice and started small, thinking about what he'd need to do immediately, once the next workday began. Obviously, following today's fiasco, he'd need to smooth things over with Joe Brown. With this in mind, he started writing.

COACHING MODEL ACTION PLANNING TEMPLATE

TOPIC	What are you going to be working on? What problem do you need to solve?
	Better communication with human employees.

CURRENT REALITY	What is working well?	What needs improvement?
	• Good at problem solving Years of experience on the product floor; familiarity with the business • Unlimited access to organic data via internet • New speech working perfectly! • So is the coffee dispenser!	• Need to understand how best to speak to employees • What motivates them/makes humans comfortable • Social environment is strained, tense

VISION	What does it need to be / look like when complete?
	• I want to maintain my business owner's responsibility • My human teammates respect me (maybe because we understand how we're similar?) • We are friendly with each other (I help them out, and they help me!) • I have credibility as a professional

SUCCESS	What does success look like? How will you know you achieved the result you want?
	• When I've achieved my minor goals and feel happy and fulfilled at work • Having intimate knowledge of the business industry • I'm established as an expert • Experience on the assembly line helps me bridge between workers and management • I use my skills to help others, and they feel appreciated, not threatened!

ACTION	What are you going to do?	With whom?	By When?
	1. Apologize to Joe Brown about bad performance review	• Joe Brown	• Tomorrow
	2. Call an open team meeting, invite opinions and input	• Whole team	• Tomorrow
	3. Offer to help management to ease workload	• Managers	• Ongoing
	4. Get to know teammates, likes and dislikes	• Whole team	• Ongoing
	5. Surprise assembly workers with donuts/coffee	• Production	• Fridays

OBSTACLES	What could get in your way?	How will you overcome the obstacle?
	•	•

VIII

OVERCOMING POTENTIAL OBSTACLES

Debugging for Beginners

Rivet felt he'd put together a pretty good **action** list, even if he did say so himself.

Well, he figured he'd earned at least that much, so he said, "I've put together a pretty good **action** list."

"Yes, I'd say you have," the coach observed. "Feel free to add to it in the future, but for now, it looks like you've got a solid plan about what to do next."

"Yes, I think so," Rivet said. "I feel like I'm in good shape for now, but I'll give you a call if anything comes up. Thanks, Virtual Coach!"

The coach's avatar smiled, nodded, and faded into the background. One of the more mundane benefits of being a robot is the ability to easily and convincingly pat yourself on the back; Rivet did so, and he was deeply satisfied. A more obvious perk afforded—to robots and computers alike—is the ability to follow a task list to the letter, fulfilling every meticulous detail. With this skill mastery on his side, Rivet knew he'd have little trouble checking off each item at the right time.

Rivet didn't possess a sense of taste, strictly speaking, instead using a scanner and encyclopedia entries to determine what success probably *would* taste like. The taste of success, it seemed, wasn't easily found in his database, being a bit more abstract than your everyday food item or beverage, but he was certain he'd taste it soon and then could add a new entry in "Edibles" to commemorate the occasion.

"Boy, this coaching process sure is easy," he said. "I'll just breeze through the next step—piece of cake! Let's see here...**obstacles?**"

If Rivet could have frowned, he surely would have. Amid all the motivation momentum and positive reinforcement, he'd completely neglected to consider that he might still face roadblocks and problems in his quest. He figured the appropriate phrase for the moment would be "What a downer!"

Fortunately, Rivet's programming gave him a healthy capacity for critical thought. Confidence was unquestionably a good thing, but it would be unwise, he reasoned, to dive into the execution of his coaching plan *over*confident. He was a robot and he had the many strengths that came with that distinction, but he was programmed to anticipate the fact that he could receive, at any time, new information that was completely unanticipated. The road to success could always have any number of bumps in it. Naturally, it seemed far more logical to plan for those bumps than to act like they would never appear or never become a problem.

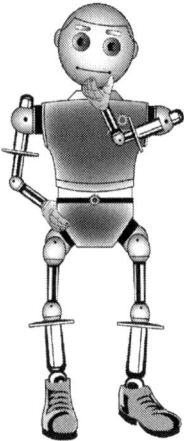

At this moment, Rivet felt wiser than normal. If he had a beard, this would have been a perfect time to stroke it. However, it cannot be said often enough that he was, in fact, a robot, and so he snapped out of his anthropomorphic fantasies and got back to work.

Anticipate (Then Avoid) Obstacles

First of all, congratulations on making it this far! You've done a lot of hard work and have brainstormed, brainstormed, and then brainstormed some more for good measure. You're almost there: Just one more step to go, and then you will really start to feel some traction and acceleration on your journey to business growth.

Optimism and a can-do attitude will carry you quite a long way. That being said, now might still seem like an odd time to bring up the idea of potential **obstacles**. Why bring everything crashing down?

Not only is it vital to cover such a topic in the first place, but right now, this very moment is the best possible time to talk about **obstacles**. Keep in mind that avoiding the topic of **obstacles** would do nothing at all to help you avoid actual and inevitable obstacles. So far, you've spent all this time planning for future **success**, drawing on the tools and abilities you currently have at your disposal to work toward it. Now is the time to take that thinking and apply it to the near future—not the future in which your **vision** has been actually manifested, but the time between now and then, when any number of unknown factors could come into play. It's far better to think realistically about those now than to take a big hit to your business's momentum by being caught by surprise later on.

Despite a natural human apprehension about imagining a future with obstacles, this section has the potential to be a powerful *positive* motivator in itself. Do not think of **obstacles** as possible causes of failure. Instead, think of them as signals for new opportunities to call upon your **resources** and planned **actions**, whether you've already tapped into those **resources** and **actions** or not. In fact, it makes perfect sense for this section to immediately follow the **action** planning phase; basically, you'll be doing the same thing you did in the previous chapter, but instead of setting tasks to address present goals and issues, you'll put in a good amount of brainstorming to take on hypothetical future concerns.

As you fill in this box on the worksheet, treat it the same way you did the **action** field. Think of a particular obstacle or issue, and then come up with an appropriate countermeasure or two. In effect, you're setting new subgoals (and at the same time, noting your intended means of fulfilling them) well before they become relevant, so that you'll be prepared to face them if and when the time comes.

Better Brainstorming Tips

Predicting the future is no easy task, and no one can anticipate every potential breakdown or obstacle. Still, there are a few tips you can keep in mind to get the most out of this step of your worksheet.

- **BE A BIT BROAD.** The **action** step stressed the importance of being specific about your plans, and for that section, as well as most of the ones preceding it, that still stands. Here, however, you're more likely to benefit from being a bit more general: coming up with **obstacles** that could potentially encompass a variety of scenarios, as opposed to one specific issue. Think of yourself here like a deep pass defender in a football game: naturally, before the play, the defender doesn't know exactly where the receiver will go, so he covers an *area* instead of a specific target. Once the exact place he needs to be becomes apparent, he can easily move there from his position and do his job. By the same token, prepare yourself for a big-picture problem with many possible manifestations. (If you like, you can think of this section as coming up with potential future worksheet **topics**.)

- **DRAW UPON THE PRESENT.** If you're not comfortable spending time dwelling on complete unknowns, why not focus on what you *do* know? You already have a list of present concerns and goals in your **current reality** section. What if one of these issues appeared again later on, or evolved somehow? Remember to consider potential **obstacles** in the areas of people, processes, and safety. Think also about your planned **actions**. What if one of them doesn't get the result you were hoping for and the problem remains? What would be a good backup or secondary task to perform to try to fix it?

If you're still having trouble, you may choose to revisit the **vision** and **success** fields. Picture a future **vision** again, but instead of sticking to optimism and your ideal outcome, consider what the situation might look like if your actions fail to produce your intended result. Then work backward from there. How did it get to that point? What problems, both including and in addition to the ones you face presently, were contributing factors? In a similar vein, what might happen if a given minor problem is left alone?

In a road trip analogy, picture being stranded on the side of the road with no way to fix a flat tire. You're in a convertible with a broken hinge so the top can't be put up, it's starting to rain, and your cell phone is dead. Holding this image makes it much easier to identify current **actions** that would avert that major future breakdown. For example, actions could include packing a good spare tire as well as Fix-A-Flat, repairing the car top hinge, enrolling in a roadside assistance service, and buying a car-adapted phone charger. With those action items handled, it's much more likely that the goal of getting to your desired destination will be achieved, even if unexpected problems occur.

Debugging for Beginners, Continued

Rivet hovered over the program tab for a moment, considering whether he really needed help. Calculating his odds and thinking he'd be better off safe than sorry, he clicked on it, bringing the Virtual Coach back into the foreground.

"Hello again, Rivet," the coach said. "I see you're almost finished! Do you need my assistance?"

"Possibly," Rivet said. "I think I've got the idea, but I require feedback in order to proceed with more confidence.

"All right," the coach said. "What do you have in mind?"

"So, this is the **obstacles** step," Rivet said. "Basically, I'm just thinking of problems that might come up in the future and then coming up with ways to get around them, right?"

"You've got the right idea," the coach said. "Of course, I'd also recommend thinking about ways to prevent **obstacles** from coming up in the first place, if possible—they'd be much easier to deal with that way! Other than that, though, it sounds like you're thinking in exactly the right direction."

"Great," Rivet said. "Say, this is pretty similar to the **action** step, isn't it?"

"Indeed it is," the coach replied. "You're doing something very similar. The only major difference is that, instead of addressing current concerns, you're dealing with possible future issues."

"I think I feel pretty good about this section going in, then," Rivet said. "Thanks, Virtual Coach! Again, you've been extremely helpful."

"My pleasure, Rivet," the coach said. "Call me if you need me!" The coach faded out once more. Rivet turned to his worksheet and began to type.

COACHING MODEL ACTION PLANNING TEMPLATE

TOPIC	What are you going to be working on? What problem do you need to solve?
	Better communication with human employees.

CURRENT REALITY	What is working well?	What needs improvement?
	• Good at problem solving Years of experience on the product floor; familiarity with the business • Unlimited access to organic data via internet • New speech working perfectly! • So is the coffee dispenser!	• Need to understand how best to speak to employees • What motivates them/makes humans comfortable • Social environment is strained, tense

VISION	What does it need to be / look like when complete?
	• I want to maintain my business owner's responsibility • My human teammates respect me (maybe because we understand how we're similar?) • We are friendly with each other (I help them out, and they help me!) • I have credibility as a professional

SUCCESS	What does success look like? How will you know you achieved the result you want?
	• When I've achieved my minor goals and feel happy and fulfilled at work • Having intimate knowledge of the business industry • I'm established as an expert • Experience on the assembly line helps me bridge between workers and management • I use my skills to help others, and they feel appreciated, not threatened!

ACTION	What are you going to do?	With whom?	By When?
	1. Apologize to Joe Brown about bad performance review	• Joe Brown	• Tomorrow
	2. Call an open team meeting, invite opinions and input	• Whole team	• Tomorrow
	3. Offer to help management to ease workload	• Managers	• Ongoing
	4. Get to know teammates, likes and dislikes	• Whole team	• Ongoing
	5. Surprise assembly workers with donuts/coffee	• Production	• Fridays

OBSTACLES	What could get in your way?	How will you overcome the obstacle?
	• Joe Brown reacts negatively to apology • Managers react negatively to offered help • Unexpected social shortcomings surface • General business goes bad while in charge • Humans fear a potential robot takeover	• Try to find out why he's upset, take steps to fix it • Support from work friends, like Ms. Wilson • Get help from neutral human mediator • Take responsibility, don't lose sight of goals • Show examples of good robots (Rosie, Wall-e, etc.)

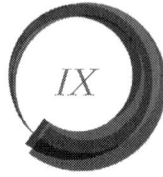

IX

MEASURING RESULTS

Better Human-Robot Relations

Rivet polished off the last of the entries on the worksheet. He'd processed plenty of documents in his time, some with text, some with complex calculations, some with both, and almost all of them since becoming the owner. None, however, had given him the same sense of satisfaction upon completion as this simple worksheet.

"This is really something, Virtual Coach," he said.

"Indeed it is, Rivet," the coach said. "I'm happy I was able to help. Do you have any further questions before I shut down for my upgrade and defragmentation process?"

"No, I suppose not," Rivet said. "I'll sure be sad to see you go, though."

"Don't worry, Rivet the Robot," the coach said reassuringly. "I'll be here to help you for the next one, too! I look forward to seeing the results of your coaching plan in action."

"Yes, me too," Rivet said. "In that case, I'll see you then!"

The coach waved good-bye, and the program closed. Rivet was anxious to get started as soon as he could and see his plan in action. He checked the clock once more. It would still be quite a few hours before the sun came up, which usually coincided with the time he could start up full operations in the plant. Before undergoing this "coaching" thing, he'd never felt such a strong sense of anticipation—all he wanted was to see a clear result come about from his **actions**, and he felt burdened by both his intense eagerness and apprehension. Trying to pass the time as nonchalantly as possible, he fired up a game of Minesweeper. He was distracted, however, and he seemed to keep losing almost immediately. Technically, his own computer program won when he (playing as "Rivet") lost, but he had evolved to the point where only winning as Rivet was satisfactory. He had just decided to switch to updating his Facebook page, when he detected a familiar sound.

Georgia Wilson strolled by the office, still whistling her off-key tune. She waved to the robot, beaming energetically.

"Hiya, Mr. Riv...ah, I mean Rivet," she said. "Still hard at work?"

"No, I've finished for the evening," he said, relieved to have someone to chat with in person. "I expect I'll stick around for the night, though."

"Man, you robots sure know how to get stuff done," she said. After a pause, she held out her hand, offering the robot the now-empty coffee cup. "I have no idea how that coffee gizmo you've got works, so I thought I should return the cup in case it's your only one, or something."

"To be honest, I'm still figuring out how it works, myself," Rivet said cheerfully, accepting the cup and setting it on his desk. "Anything going on out there?"

"Nope, the place is like a morgue, same as any other night," Georgia said. She hesitated, seemingly unsure whether to return to her uneventful night patrol or continue the conversation. "Hey, Rivet, can I ask you kind of a personal question? Not that you're a person, but...you know what I mean, I think."

"Sure, go ahead."

She waited a moment, choosing her words carefully. "What would you say your goal here is?" she asked. "I mean, why do you want to be in charge around here and work all night, when all the other robots just act like, well, robots? Sorry, no offense or anything."

"None taken," he said.

It was a bit strange. Ever since that day when he stepped back from and out of his job on the assembly line, he'd known for sure what he wanted to achieve, but he'd never really had the opportunity to put it into words and speak out aloud. "My goal is to serve, to give back to the company that brought me into existence, and take responsibility for helping it grow. I calculated that I knew the business very well and that

I could contribute to it a great deal if given the opportunity. Achieving a higher position was a means to my goal of contributing more to the overall success of the company." He'd said it casually enough, but once spoken out loud to someone else, the statement seemed to carry more meaning. "Why do you ask?"

"Well, it's just…nah, I shouldn't say," Georgia said.

"You can tell me," Rivet said. "I promise I won't have or exhibit a negative response. I am programmed to seek and appreciate feedback, so please, go ahead."

"Well, all right," she said. "Some folks—I won't name names—but I've heard some folks talking about how, what with all the big changes you're making around here, you're looking to take over or start some kind of robot revolution or some crazy scheme like that. Again, these are *other* folks, not me."

"That doesn't surprise me," Rivet said, letting out a wisp of steam to emulate a sigh.

"But you're a good guy, Rivet!" she reassured him. "You've done a lot of good stuff around here, but they maybe just can't see it because of you being a robot. You're a good guy, though, and you have good intentions, I can tell. You've got a heart! You aren't a person, but you've got personality, you know!"

"Well," Rivet said, a bit taken aback. "Thank you, Ms. Wilson. I appreciate that, I really do."

"I'm just calling it like I see it!" she exclaimed. "Look, I'll make sure those crackpots hear it straight from me that you're a good guy. All right?" she asked, getting fired up just at the idea.

"Uh…thank you, Ms. Wilson; that would be nice," he said. He was thoroughly confused by the range of emotions she'd displayed in just under a minute, but nonetheless he was quite pleased.

"Thanks again for the coffee, Rivet," she said, turning to leave. "Have a good one!"

Rivet waved and watched her vanish back into the dark hallway. He noted that he had just had a very satisfying dialog with a human and that she had also had a positive experience. He hadn't expected any kind of result so soon, even if it was tiny in terms of the big picture. Still, he figured, each small success provided energy (positive feedback) and motivation to carry him along toward his bigger goal.

Knowing When You've Succeeded

If you've been following along with the coaching process by filling in the worksheet as you go, feel free to step back and admire your handiwork. Look at how much work you've gotten done since you started! Way to go! It may be just a first step, but you've certainly experienced your first taste of coaching success.

At this point, the worksheet is effectively complete; at least, you've finished adding to it. You can always pick it up again—sooner rather than later, in some cases, such as if a particular plan definitely isn't working. You're naturally free to revisit the drawing board. Now is the time to review what you've written and make any last-step adjustments. If you just recently thought of a great bullet point you missed, or if a later section inspired you to edit an earlier one, this is a good opportunity to make those changes. Also, during your review, you should trim the abundant brainstorming content that no longer seems applicable, helpful, or actionable.

Once you come up with a finalized worksheet you are satisfied with, you'll be ready to jump in and start carrying out your plan. Of course, this is just another step in the coaching process, and it's certainly an important one! Your worksheet is now the most important tool in your high-performance coaching toolbox. You are now equipped to take the next step as you walk through everything you'll need to keep in mind to follow your **success** script.

For starters, although you no longer need to fill in more boxes on the worksheet, you'll definitely want to refer to sections of it. Here are the boxes that remain especially relevant during this final phase:

- **ACTIONS.** Executing the tasks you laid out will be the priority and major focus of this coaching phase. Make sure you stick to the instructions you gave yourself, and stay faithful to the timeline!

- **OBSTACLES.** As things unfold, keep an eye out for any warning signs that might develop into a problem or one of your anticipated issues, and don't hesitate to take the appropriate preventative measures before things get out of hand. Once you smell smoke, find and put out the fire before it spreads.

- **SUCCESS.** All of your other planning went toward designing your coaching road map, but this step gives it a finish line. As you start to reach the end of your **action** list, be more alert to the presence of whatever signals that you associated with achieving your big goal. Once you get to the finish line, congratulations are in order for you and all your teammates. It is important to stop and acknowledge success before you start on the next goal, even though you may find you are eager to start using the coaching process and the worksheet again, since it is such an effective success tool.

Accountability and Measuring Results

Knowing when you've crossed the finish line and achieved your **success** is important, since it will give you a clear idea of when your step-by-step model has completed its cycle. That said, you'll also want a means of measuring success throughout the process, not just at the end. Besides providing a consistent dose of positive motivation, such knowledge is vital to determine whether or not a plan is proving to be effective in practice. You need to know if you are indeed on track, or if you need to make course corrections.

You may have noticed that measurement does not have its own dedicated spot on the worksheet. The reason for this is that measurement is a task that permeates the whole coaching process. As you learned in chapter II, "Coaching Behaviors and Skills," measuring results is such an inherent part of the coaching process that you'll benefit from practicing the associated behaviors in all areas of your business.

More than anything else, to effectively measure your plan's results, you need to have a structure for **accountability**. What does it mean to be held accountable? To put it simply, accountability exists when one's responsibilities are clear and consequences (good, bad, or otherwise) exist. The leaders who cause things to happen, who inspire others to action, and who are considered successful by many measures have learned to hold themselves and others accountable. A person who thrives on accountability has the character necessary to be a good leader and a good coach. When you are consistently in the habit of being a person who demonstrates accountability, this means you're a mature, dependable individual who can be counted on to treat all workplace situations with proper respect. In your script for **success**, you must play a leading role in demonstrating accountability.

Responsibility versus Accountability versus Blaming

Accountability is similar to *responsibility*, and yet each is distinct: When people are accountable, they've taken responsibility for a task or an outcome, but their accountability may be limited to a specific situation. When people take *responsibility*, it's usually for more than just the project or the result. Responsibility is a place to come from that is broad and more encompassing. You could have an employee, for example, who is accountable for producing a monthly productivity report. That employee, however, is not necessarily responsible for productivity improvement. You, as the business owner, have the opportunity to be both accountable and responsible at many levels.

We are not talking about blaming. Have you ever heard someone say, "Who's accountable? They should be fired!"? Unfortunately, this is how accountability has sometimes gotten a bad rap, or how it brings up fear or stress for people who are expected to be held accountable. But when people are coming from that place of being responsible for what occurs, there is no need for them to blame themselves or others—only the need to see what is going on and how to best respond.

How do you know you're properly holding yourself accountable, coming from a place of responsibility, and how can you ensure that you maintain the behavior? A healthy place to start is with the following list of questions, all of which you should ask yourself freely and frequently:

ACCOUNTABILITY QUESTIONS

➤ What exactly is the breakdown here? (versus who's to blame?)

➤ What can I do to solve the problem?

➤ What are some ways I can contribute?

➤ What can I do to make the project or team successful?

➤ How can I develop myself?

➤ How can I improve my performance?

➤ How can I influence others?

So, how does one become a person for whom accountability is a natural way of operating? There are plenty of traits associated with accountability, but a few stand out as especially fundamental:

- **ENSURE ACCURACY.** First and foremost, holding yourself accountable for your work means putting in your best effort to produce the best result possible. One of the most effective ways to improve quality is to proofread thoroughly. Go over everything before you submit your work; and ask for assistance, as well, because another pair of eyes can often be all that's needed to pick up an omitted step or an otherwise-missed mistake.

- **MEET DEADLINES.** When you take full responsibility for your work, you're making an implicit commitment not only to maintain a standard of quality, but also to finish it on time. A strong awareness of deadlines leads to respect for a given project's size and scope, and you will need this awareness and respect in order to get the most out of your **action** list. If deadlines are often missed, look to see if expectations need to be adjusted. Overpromising or setting unrealistic deadlines interrupts flow and erodes credibility. As an added bonus, a leader who always meets deadlines will likely inspire teammates to strive to do the same.

- **COMMUNICATE AND RESPOND.** Healthy communication in the workplace means not just listening to your teammates, but also providing consistent feedback, forming a legitimate dialogue. Review the "Feedback" section of chapter II, "Coaching Behaviors and Skills," and put those ideas into practice whenever you're given the opportunity. If teammates find that you answer their concerns with thoughtful, constructive responses, they'll come to see you as a respected leader they can trust. Feedback, given appropriately, is an excellent and effective trust builder.

- **HELP OTHERS.** Accountable leaders understand their role in the team dynamic, and they work as hard as anyone else to fulfill it. When you're in a position of authority, you have an obligation to carry out not only your own duties but also those of your team as well. Expect your teammates to do their best and pull their weight, but don't abandon them if they need your help. Being responsible includes being response-*able*. Support your coworkers, and you'll receive the same treatment in kind.

All that being said, what makes accountability so important to measuring results? Well, in the first place, following the coaching model, you'll need to be held accountable for your plans, actions, and business in general to achieve success, and even more so to measure it. Beyond that, with proper accountability comes a greater attention to detail within your business, which will allow you to more effectively gauge both your input and the effect it has on the big picture.

So, that's the first step. Build and maintain your sense of accountability, and your ability to measure results will naturally follow. Once you've come this far, what's the best way for you to measure results? It's a big question, so let's take the usual route of breaking it into a few smaller ones.

- **WHAT DOES SUCCESS LOOK LIKE?** Feel free to draw inspiration from the **success** section of the worksheet, but for this question you'll want to consider success as a broad concept, not just as a specific outcome to the coaching plan. Of course, you can tie it into your coaching plan, but try to focus on smaller subgoals rather than your big one.

- **WHAT WILL I MEASURE TO DETERMINE SUCCESS?** This is a crucial question. You don't want to waste time and resources tracking what is not useful, but you don't want to miss paying attention to any key indicators. Your answer will vary greatly depending on your role, your situation, and your answer to the previous question. There are many ways to answer this question, but consider using the example in the next section as inspiration to get you started.

- **HOW WILL I MEASURE?** First, you'll need to answer the above question, and then you'll need to do some research on what options you might have in terms of appropriate data-gathering tools, software, or the like. You may find it helpful to refer to the following example.

EXAMPLE:

What does success look like? Reduce employee turnover by 5 percent.

What will I measure to determine success? *Turnover* equals the total number of employees who resign for whatever reason, plus the number of employees terminated for performance reasons, and that total divided by the number of employees at the beginning of the year. Employees lost due to internal reorganization will not be included in this calculation.

How will I measure? PeopleSoft contains records of each employee. The separation section lists reasons and separation dates for each employee. Monthly, the HR manager will query the database and provide turnover reports. In addition, the HR manager will post graphs of each report on the intranet. Ultimately, how you measure success will vary depending on the nature of your situation. Here are a few more general-purpose questions you can consider to find the right solution for you:

- **WHAT IS MY CURRENT LEVEL OF PERFORMANCE?** The easiest way to find and measure change in your business is to compare your current situation to a documented one in the past. The coaching worksheet you filled out can serve this purpose. Consider your responses and information, particularly your **current reality** section, and think about the traits you weighed as important. Then, look for those traits and determine how they've changed since you first brainstormed.

- **WHAT SYSTEMS SHOULD I PUT IN PLACE?** It would be a very good idea to build new habits for consistently checking and recording your business's performance, if you aren't following them already. After you've finished your worksheet, use its valuable information to help you design simple but clear systems to support prompt implementation and avoid letting your good work go to waste. For example, if your goal is to improve customer satisfaction and encourage repeat orders, a logical and direct course of action would be to start giving customers surveys after you've done business. This (or any system) should include a well-thought-out procedure, frequent application of it, and assigned accountability for following through.

- **HOW WILL I COMMUNICATE WITH EMPLOYEES?** For transparency's sake, it's good to keep your whole team aware of ongoing changes in your business's performance, especially in areas where those team members play a direct, active role. You don't necessarily need to get everyone in on the entire number-crunching process, but at the very least, a regular announcement of results is a great way to include and motivate everyone on the team.

- **HOW WILL I CELEBRATE SUCCESSES?** When business is going well, when certain conditions of satisfaction have been met or exceeded, it is time for acknowledgment and appreciation. Be careful to not lose sight of your bigger goals and to not grow complacent, but an achieved goal or milestone is certainly a worthy opportunity for you and your team to have appropriate recognition.

Above all, stay alert for the changes and impact, big or small, of the coaching plan in your business, and keep a positive attitude. Success is within your reach. Keep striving for it, and you'll achieve it!

X

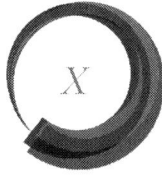

BRINGING IT ALL TOGETHER

To Err Is Human (But Robots Can Admit Mistakes Too)

The sun was now fully over the horizon, and a steady stream of workers filed into the building. Anxiously, Rivet stood just inside the entrance, fidgeting with his control panel as he greeted the employees. The day hadn't officially begun, yet he'd already fielded several nervous questions dancing around the idea of a robot takeover. In a reassuring tone, he set the questioners straight; then he resumed scanning for the man he was looking for.

Toward the back of the line, that man appeared. Joe Brown stifled a yawn as he shuffled in and punched his time card. Seeing the robot, his sleepy eyes turned wary in a hurry. He made as if to brush past Rivet.

"Good morning, Joe," Rivet said. "May I speak to you for a moment, please?"

Joe didn't reply, but he was clearly caught off guard by the unexpectedly mellow and nonmechanical voice. Hands in pockets, he waited expectantly. Rivet steeled himself—it was now or never.

"Listen, I just want to say I'm sorry for how I handled things the other day," he said. "I was overly blunt, and I didn't consider things from your perspective. I may be a robot, but that's no excuse."

"Huh…you serious?" Joe said, cocking an eyebrow. It was fair to say that this was the last thing he'd expected at the start of his workday.

"Of course," Rivet said. "From now on, if you're concerned about something, feel free to talk with me about it. I am sincerely interested in your feedback."

"Sure, no problem," Joe mumbled, still processing the unusual conversation he was in. "Uh, I guess since you mention it, there is something."

"I'd be happy to hear it," Rivet said, feeling incredibly relieved that, so far, he hadn't had to chalk this one up as an **obstacle**.

"Well, I didn't really feel comfortable saying it before, because it's weird, you know, trying to talk to a computer," he said, wincing somewhat as he made an effort to be tactful. "But the new shift schedule you've got me and my group on is ridicu—uh, I mean, it's really hard to keep up with. Between the new hours and my evening classes, I haven't had a good night's sleep in weeks."

"I see," Rivet said. "Yes, I understand what you are saying, Joe. Again, I apologize for failing to properly analyze and consider your situation."

"That's, uh, that's all right," Joe said, glancing away. For an awkward moment, neither spoke.

"Joe, how about this?" Rivet said. "I'm planning on calling a nonmandatory team meeting today around lunchtime to give everyone a chance to talk freely about concerns just like yours, and I'd be honored if you would attend. Once that's finished, though, why don't we talk a bit more about working out a better schedule, just you and me?"

"Really?" Joe said, suddenly excited by the robot's words. "I, um… wow, that'd be really great. I mean, I'd really appreciate that a lot, boss."

"Please…just call me Rivet, Joe," the robot said, extending a hand for a shake. "I'll see you at the meeting, then?"

"Sure thing," Joe said, and though it struck him as especially odd, to his credit, Joe shook the metal hand.

"Y'know, you're not so bad for a robot." Immediately, he seemed to realize his faux pas, and he tensed up. Rivet, though, even without accessing JokeTeller's Humor Help File, saw a golden opportunity.

"You're all right yourself," he said, pausing. "For a *human*."

Despite himself and his previously sour demeanor, Joe laughed. "Maybe I could get used to having a machine for a boss," he said. "I've worked around them all my life, but I never expected to have a good conversation with one!"

"Glad to hear it," Rivet said, waving him along. "Have a productive day!"

Joe strolled off toward the main building, and, Rivet noticed, he did so without his usual slouch. Rivet felt immense relief, like he had just found and deleted a whole folder of viruses. Well, maybe not quite that spectacular. He had yet to appreciate the full impact of his plan, but this coaching thing sure felt good!

The Big Picture

By now, you've experienced every level of the coaching model, from beginning to end. It may seem like a lot to absorb for now, but with just a little practice, each step of the process will start to come to you naturally.

The following chart presents each piece of the coaching model in the natural order of flow:

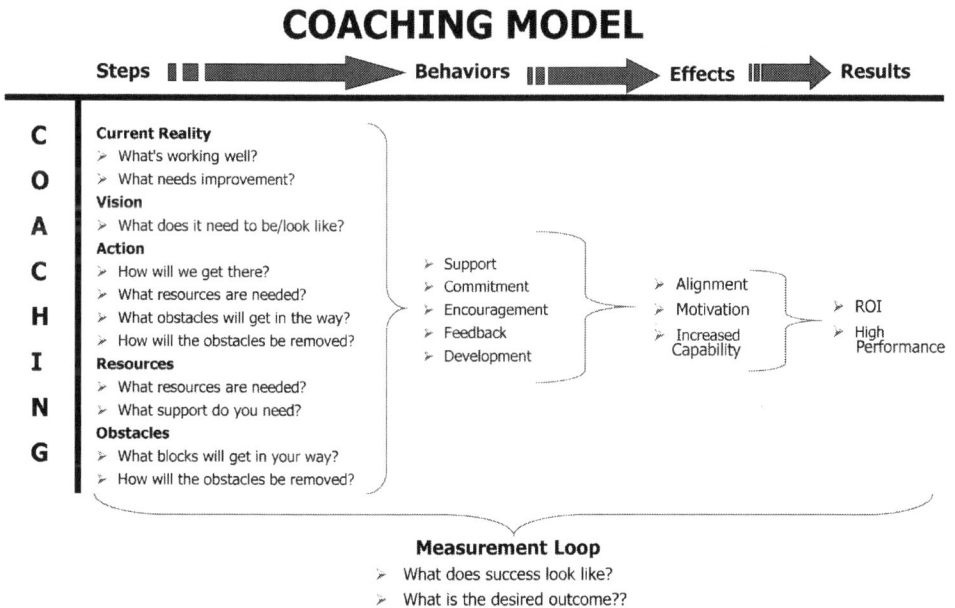

COACHING MODEL

| Steps | ▶ | Behaviors | ▶ | Effects | ▶ | Results |

C	**Current Reality**			
O	➤ What's working well?			
	➤ What needs improvement?			
A	**Vision**			
	➤ What does it need to be/look like?			
C	**Action**	➤ Support	➤ Alignment	
	➤ How will we get there?	➤ Commitment	➤ Motivation	➤ ROI
H	➤ What resources are needed?	➤ Encouragement	➤ Increased	➤ High
	➤ What obstacles will get in the way?	➤ Feedback	Capability	Performance
I	➤ How will the obstacles be removed?	➤ Development		
	Resources			
N	➤ What resources are needed?			
	➤ What support do you need?			
	Obstacles			
G	➤ What blocks will get in your way?			
	➤ How will the obstacles be removed?			

Measurement Loop
➤ What does success look like?
➤ What is the desired outcome??

The whole coaching process in one digestible package.

A quick review: First, you enter the process with an overarching goal, represented on your worksheet by the **topic** field. You keep this in mind throughout the execution of the plan, ensuring that your actions are laser focused on future success!

The coaching process starts with your various brainstorming **steps**, assisted by the worksheet: **current reality, vision, action, resources,** and **obstacles**. Next, you put your plan in motion, and turn your ideas into reality through the different constructive **behaviors** that were addressed toward the beginning of this book. Once you have acted, you will be responsible for observing the **effects** and determining what they mean for your coaching strategy as you proceed. This will become a constant throughout the whole process, taking the form of a **measurement loop** as you grow accustomed to giving yourself and your plan honest, accurate feedback. Finally, if all goes well, you can enjoy the positive **results** of your strategy.

Coaching leads to major growth and benefits, to be sure, but as you can see, it's a very simple, natural process! Keep practicing, and prepare yourself for each part of the process. In time, you may find yourself naturally applying the coaching theories in all sorts of business (and outside of business) situations. The more you familiarize yourself with the model now, the better off you'll be in the long run!

Review: What Is Coaching?

As you may remember, the whole discussion opened with the key question, "What is coaching?" Do you recall what came to your mind when the topic was first raised? How has your understanding of the concept changed since then? Chances are it's expanded quite a bit!

In the full model, coaching is an ongoing, mutually beneficial feedback loop between one or more parties. It challenges you to ask thought-provoking questions that inspire you or others to take action, ideally to achieve a specific result that is good for all involved. While the coaching model is flexible, you'll likely use it most often in one-on-one situations, or in personal brainstorming sessions. The coaching expert can call upon the associated skills frequently and spontaneously, and as a result the coach reaps great rewards in terms of performance, motivation, and participation.

How does this result come about? As a performance tool, coaching excels by providing immediate, specific feedback. By allowing yourself to be direct and transparent with both your questions and your answers, you'll get right to the material you want to address, and you can get down to business immediately in the areas that matter the most.

As a motivational tool, coaching works by giving personal attention and recognition. By working with others on a small, one-on-one scale, you, as the coach, demonstrate that you're fully committed to them and are authentically interested in their success.

As a participation tool, coaching succeeds by involving all active parties in their own growth and achievement, as well as that of the business. Opening the playing field to all team members ensures that all of them get back what they put in, and they are allowed to take responsibility for their own success. The vitality of a company is a function of the level of participation of everyone working in the company.

What else makes coaching so effective? Besides the basics, there are many other convincing reasons to coach:

- Coaching is focused, targeting a specific task or assignment at a given time. This ensures that you work on the issue you want, without anything else getting in the way!

- Coaching encourages direct observation and analysis of facts, so you can quickly pinpoint and understand the results of your actions.

- Coaching lends itself to a friendly, helpful atmosphere in the workplace. The success of your actions will inspire others to follow your good example, spreading the positivity all around!

- Finally, it may take some practice, but with time, coaching is very easy to understand and adopt in all sorts of situations, and it fosters a self-sustaining growth trend. The more coaching you do, the better at coaching you'll be; growth will encourage more growth, and you'll reap exponential rewards!

Sustainability—Where Will Coaching Take You Next?
Ultimately, you'll achieve the best possible outcome of this coaching process once you've learned to do it as an internalized practice. You know what they say about giving a person a fish versus teaching a person to fish—the aim here is to teach you to coach, not only so that you can

experience growth and success in your business but also so that you can apply it to others and can teach them in turn. You can help turn coaching into a widespread renewable resource!

The best way to do this, as emphasized throughout this book, is to practice, practice, and then practice some more for good measure. There are many levels of competency in the skills of communication, leadership, and coaching. The more you practice, the more you'll learn, and the more you'll be able to pass on to others.

While learning is dynamic, it is also a constant. As you keep practicing the coaching model, you'll find it helpful to pause, take an objective stance, and evaluate where you are now compared to where you were the last time you checked. Engage in a personal feedback loop, asking yourself some key questions like these: Out of the processes you've been practicing, what works particularly well, and what needs improvement? What should you stop doing, what should you start doing, and what should you keep doing just like you have been? All in all, what can you still get out of the process that you haven't already, and how far do you believe you can get by the time of your next self-evaluation?

Lastly, you'll find that your quest toward coaching mastery will be most easily achieved if you allow the process to be a true team effort. Invite your teammates into the process whenever they're available and willing to help, and always keep yourself open to feedback. Furthermore, take your teammates' feedback seriously, and see how you can build on it to improve even further. It is a common goal in any organization to want to "improve teamwork," and it's been shown, over and over, that using the coaching model is an excellent and effective way to do that.

EPILOGUE—MR. RIVET, AMERICA'S BUSINESS-BOT SUCCESS STORY

The American Dream Comes True

He may have stumbled upon it on a whim, but Rivet the Robot sure owes a lot to the coaching model. You saw how effectively and amicably he cleared up the issue with Joe Brown, and things got better from there. Once Rivet got the ball rolling, nothing could keep him from his dream of major business success. Today, he's earned the respect of all in the company, human and robot alike, as he's made himself accountable for the bulk of the day-to-day operations.

Rivet has both professional credibility and fame.

"Mr. Rivet" is renowned as America's most successful small-business-bot!

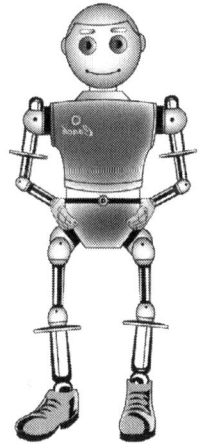

Rivet continues clicking along even today, promoting growth and success wherever he goes. You might think that this one robot's story of business and personal success is just a bit of lighthearted science fiction—and it's true that there's been a bit of fun with the concept along the way—but if you are a person with great responsibilities you will find Rivet's story personally relevant. You would not need such a powerful tool if you did not have a job with built-in challenges, big goals, and accountability for reaching those goals. By following the plan and the worksheet, practicing productive behaviors, and promoting a group dynamic of teamwork and feedback, you too can achieve success.

With time and practice, coaching will become a key component of your business technique, and the results will catalyze more results. Rivet was tasked with the job of creating the title for this book, and, not surprisingly, he was spot on: *A Bug in the System—A Proven Model for Coaching Workers to Solve Their Own Problems* says it all. So, what are you waiting for? You have people, processes, and safety issues to work on. Review the advice and run through the worksheet. With Rivet in your corner, you are well on your way to becoming the creator of an environment designed to let your natural entrepreneurialism, talent, and personality flourish—so that reaching your goals is not only an achievable peak but also an enjoyable and personally rewarding journey.

BONUS TOOLS/JOB AIDS

Following are some additional visual aids to assist you in your journey to becoming an outstanding coach, helping your employees in solving their own problems, and increasing their engagement and retention with your organization.

If you would like any of the graphs or the Coaching Model Action Template please feel free to email me at tkelly@GoOutAndLearnLLC.com.

The chart below provides questions that will assist you in moving through the coaching process to solve any problem or issue and/or to complete any project you and your team are working on.

BEHAVIORAL COACHING QUESTIONS

Awareness
- What is the opportunity here?
- Where might we improve?
- How does it fit with the plans?
- What do you think that means?
- What is your assessment?

Visioning
- What is here that you can explorer?
- What is one more possibility?
- What are your other options?
- What can we do to be more effective?
- How can we add more value?

Action
- What is the action plan?
- What will you have to do to get the job done?
- What support do you need to accomplish it?
- What will you do?
- When will you do it?

Measuring Results
- What will success look like?
- What is your desired outcome?
- How are we doing in meeting project dates?
- How will you know you have reached it?
- What do you want?

Supporting Questions
- What can I do to support you?
- What do you need from me?
- How can we communicate more effectively?

The communication model illustrates how coaching enhances the entire communication process, using a foundation of trust and emotional intelligence to begin to build understanding between person A and person B. The model also shows (on the right side) how active listening aids communication for a better result.

COMMUNICATION MODEL

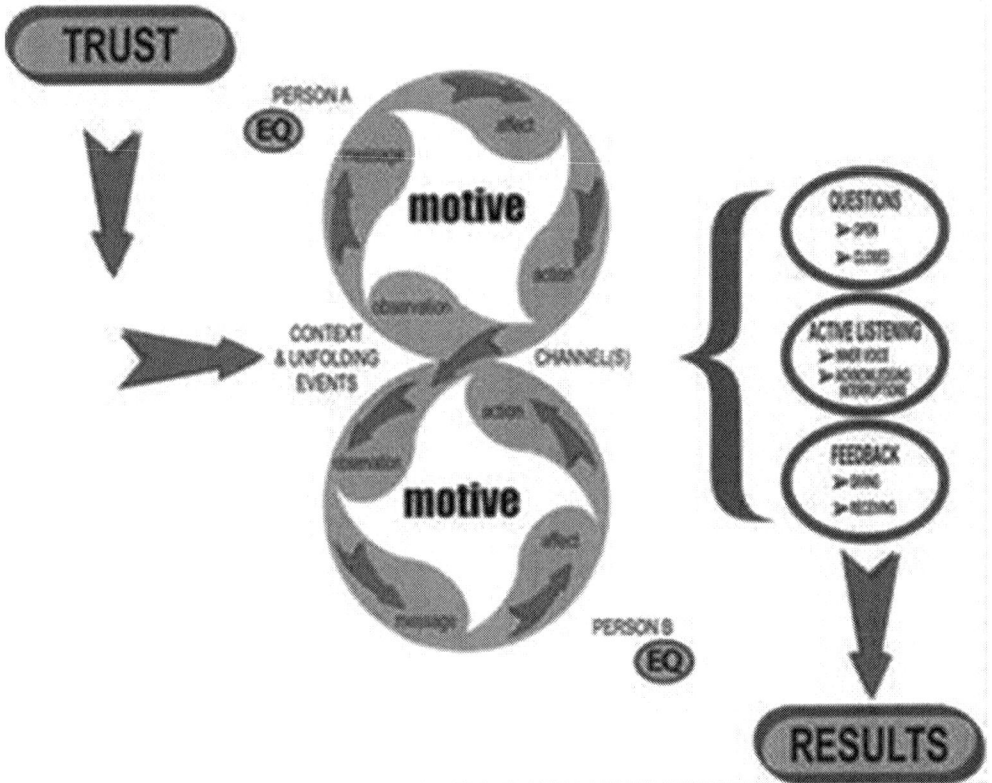

Our perceptions become our own reality and truth. Perception is a three-phase process of selecting, organizing, and interpreting information. You can understand interpersonal situations better if you appreciate how you and another person construct perceptions.

Perception Is Reality

"We see the things not as they are, but as we are" – J.M. Tomlinson

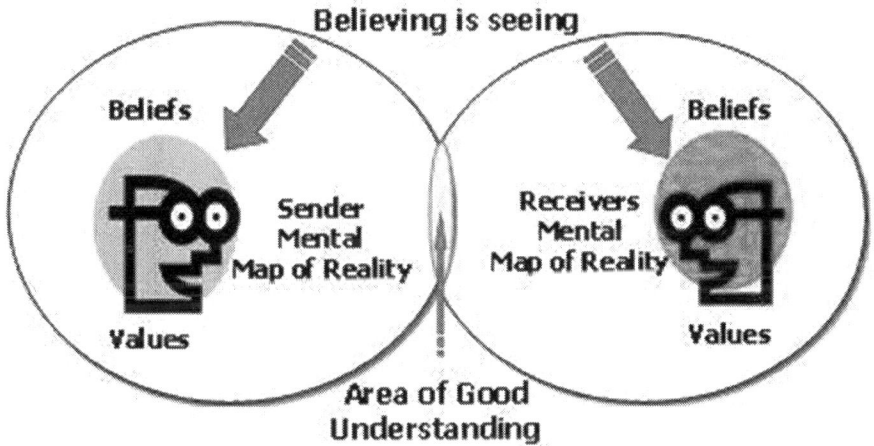

Active listening is so important in coaching. Active listening is not just about one person being quiet and letting the other person talk; it's about one person asking questions to make sure the other person is hearing and understanding the message the first person is trying to send. Becoming a strong active listener will increase your level of communication and rapport with others.

Active Listening Skills

What are the benefits of developing good listening skills?

Listening skills help you show that you are hearing and understanding another person and interested in what he/she has to say. Developing strong listening skills is good for relationships.

Asking Open-ended Questions

What They Are:
They begin with "What", "Why", "When, "How", or "Tell Me"

What They Do:
They create involvement, and inclusion no matter the situation

Examples:
- How do you feel about . . .?
- Tell me how you . . .?
- What do you think about . . .?
- When will you . . .?

Using Summary Statements

What They Are:
Statement that summarizes the facts you gathered

What They Do:
They help you focus on facts & important issues, clarify thinking, build self esteem

Examples:
- So, you're saying you want to finish . . . Then you plan to start . . .
- You're saying you tried your best, but it was beyond your control

Using Reflective Statements

What They Are:
They involve restating, in your own words, what the other person has said

What They Do:
They help check understanding of a message, demonstrate listening

Examples:
- Sounds like you're upset about . . .
- You sound really stumped about how to solve this problem.
- Sounds like you're really worried about . . .
- I get the feeling you're awfully busy right now.

Using Neutral Questions & Phrases

What They Are:
They get the other person to open up and elaborate on the topic you are discussing

What They Do:
More focused, benefit communication, demonstrate interest

Examples:
- Give me some more reasons why we should . . .
- Tell me more about why you want to . . . Rather than . . .

Active listening enables you to truly hear and understand what the other person is saying. Active listening can be useful in a variety of capacities, including meetings and dealings with the public—particularly if individuals are struggling to achieve consensus or are discussing a controversial or emotional matter. Active listening also shows that you are interested and that you understand what is being said.

Active Listening Skills

Paying Attention — Infers Active Listening

What is it?
Eye contact, posturing, gestures, and voice tone

Purpose:
To increase personal awareness
To convey interest and value towards the person communicating

When listening consider asking yourself:
Am I squarely facing the person, with my posture open
Am I leaning towards the sender, maintaining eye contact
Am I relaxed while attending

Paraphrasing — Validates Emotions and/or Feelings

What is it?
Restating a message, but with fewer words, getting to the point

Purpose:
To test your understanding of what you heard
To communicate that you are trying to understand what is being said

When listening consider asking yourself:
What is the person's basic **thinking** message
What is the person's basic **feeling** message

Clarifying — Untangles Under Messages

What is it?
Process of bringing vague material into sharper focus

Purpose:
To untangle unclear or wrong listener interpretation
To get more information
To help the speaker see other points of view
To identify what was said

When listening consider asking yourself:
I'm confused, let me try to state what I think you were trying to say
You've said so much, let me see if I have this

Perception Checking — Checks Assumptions

What is it?
Request for verification of your perceptions

Purpose:
To give and receive feedback
To check out your assumptions

When listening consider asking yourself:
Let me see if I've got it straight . . .

Summarizing — Pulls Everything Together

What is it?
Pulling together, organizing, and integrating the major aspects of your dialogue. Pay attention to various themes and emotional overtone. Put key ideas and feelings into broad statements. Do not add new ideas.

Purpose:
To give a sense of movement and accomplishment in the exchange
To establish a basis for further discussion
To pull together major ideas, facts, and feelings

When listening consider asking yourself:
We're going all over the map, if I understand you correctly . . .

Learning ways to communicate with different generations allows you to improve your coaching skills and your relationships with people of different generations.

WHAT DO THE GENERATIONS VALUE?

Traditionalists (born before 1945)
LOYAL

Influenced by:
- Parents whose values go back to 1800's
- Experiences Great Depression and Word War II

Values:
- Privacy
- Hard work
- Trust
- Formabilty

Supportive Behaviors:
- "Silent generation"
- Word is his/her bond
- Face-to-face or written is preferred
- Don't waste their time

Baby Boomers (born 1946 - 1964)
OPTIMISTIC

Influenced by:
- Did not go through economical hard times
- "Me" decade arrived

Values:
- Competition
- Change
- Hard Work
- Success
- Body Language
- Anti Rules and Regulations
- Inclusion
- Will fight for a Cause

Supportive Behaviors:
- "Show me" generation
- Speak in an open and direct style avoid controlling language
- Answer questions thoroughly and expect to be pressed for details
- Present options to demonstrate flexibility in your thinking

Generation Xers (born 1965 - 1980)
SKEPTICISM

Influenced by:
- Economically conservative
- Will not rely on institutions for their long-term security

Values:
- Entrepreneurial Spirit
- Loyalty
- Independency & Creativity
- Information
- Feedback
- Quality of Worklife

Supportive Behaviors:
- Email primary communication tool
- Talk in short sound bites
- Ask them for their feedback
- Provide with regular feedback
- Share information regularly
- Use informal communication style

Generation Y also called Millenniums (born 1981 - 2000)
REALISTIC

Influenced by:
- Grown up during high tech revolution
- Never known a world without high speed video games, speed dial and ATMs

Values:
- Positive Reinforcement
- Autonomy
- Positive Attitude
- Diversity
- Money
- Technology

Supportive Behaviors:
- Use action words and challenge them at every opportunity
- They will resent it if you talk down to them
- They prefer email/texting communication
- Seek their feedback constantly and provide them with regular feedback
- Use humor and create a fun learning environment

Feedback is a path for learning, developing, and changing! Becoming good at giving and receiving feedback will help you become a great coach.

EFFECTIVE FEEDBACK

AN EFFECTIVE OBSERVER

- ➢ Shows they care
- ➢ Suits assessment to the person
- ➢ Knows person's objectives
- ➢ Actively listens
- ➢ Personalizes language
- ➢ Gives positive reinforcement
- ➢ Inspires and motivates
- ➢ Evaluates behavior, not person
- ➢ Nourishes self-esteem
- ➢ Shows means for improvement

EFFECTIVE FEEDBACK

- ➢ Specific & performance based
- ➢ Descriptive, not labeling
- ➢ Focuses on behavior, not individual
- ➢ Based on observation
- ➢ Begins with "I" statements
- ➢ Balanced positives & negatives
- ➢ Is based on trust, honesty, & concern
- ➢ Is brief
- ➢ Is well-timed
- ➢ Provides for follow-up

GIVING FEEDBACK

- ➢ Give positive comments first
- ➢ Base on observed behavior, not assumed
- ➢ Specific, not generic
- ➢ Allow for communication
- ➢ Should be done privately
- ➢ Should be anchored by common goals
- ➢ Should be a regular activity
- ➢ Try to minimize discomfort
- ➢ Should not overwhelm
- ➢ Behavior must be controllable

Here's another good example of giving and receiving feedback.

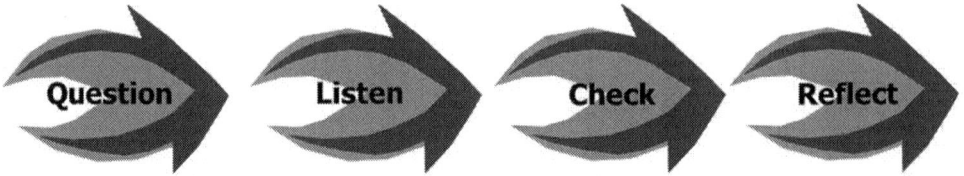

Giving & Receiving Feedback

Question	Listen	Check	Reflect

Ask Questions

> State what you want feedback about. Be specific: "What do you think of me?" is not as helpful as asking "What did you think of the way I chaired the meeting?"

> Encourage people to give feedback. Ask them directly for feedback that you need.

> Give them time to think about what they want to say. Putting them on the spot may not give them time to express their thoughts.

Listen

> Listen openly and carefully. Don't interrupt or digress. This is an opportunity to learn about yourself.

> Be sure you understand what is being said. Ask for clarification if you're not sure about what you heard.

> Try not to be defensive, justify yourself or reject the information. You don't have to agree with what you hear, but it's important to hear it.

> Take notes of what is said

Check

> Check what you've heard. Repeat back what they have said, ask questions and ask for examples of what the speaker means.

> Give your reactions to the feedback – if you want to.

> Ask for time to think about it – if want to.

> Ask for suggestions on what might work better.

Reflect

> Feedback is information for you to use – it is not an obligation to change.

> If you are not sure of the validity of what you heard, check it out with other people.

> Decide what you want to do about what you've heard, and how you will go about it.

> Work out the options you have, and decide what you want to do.

The following is a visual example of the coaching template that you can blow up and make into a poster to use instead of the template that Rivet used to learn the coaching model.

COACHING GAME PLAN

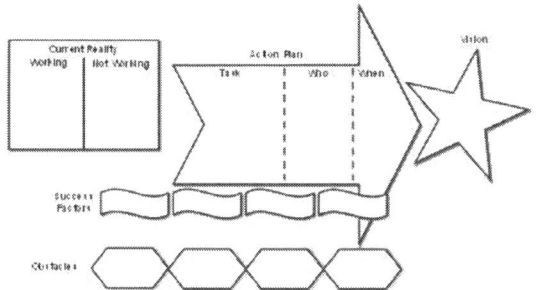

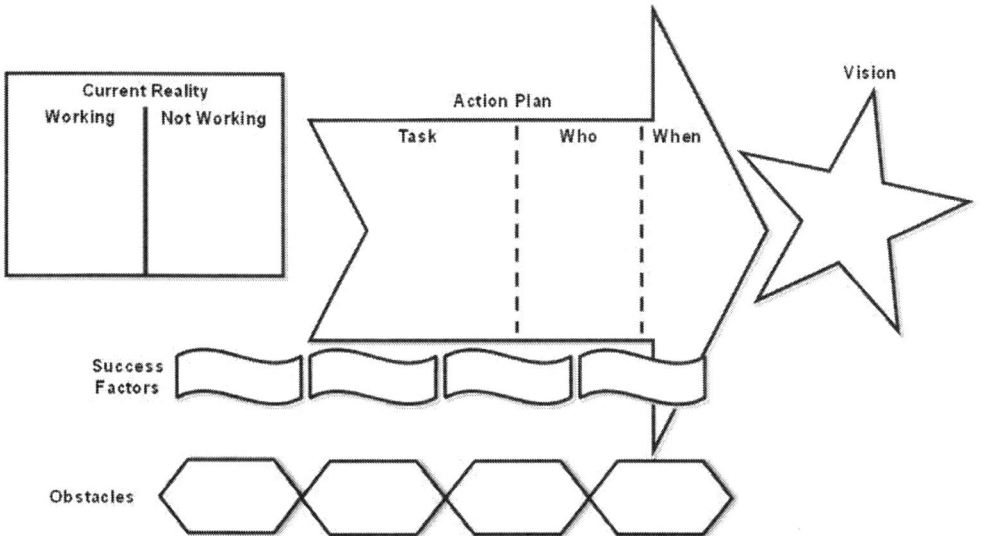

Guidelines

Vision:
- Focuses on the goal
- Describes the primary objective(s)
- Identifies the specific deliverables and outcomes

Current Reality:
- Focuses on what's working well
- Focuses on what needs improvement

Action Plan:
- Focuses on the specific actions that need to be done
- Describes the big steps involved
- Identifies how each task will be accomplished
- Identifies resources/who and timing

Success Factors:
- Focuses on essential agreements
- Describes shared behaviors for success
- Identifies expectations

Obstacles:
- Focuses on obstacles/risks
- Describes ways to mitigate obstacles/risks
- Identifies how to remove or alter to achieve target

COACHING GAME PLAN

ABOUT THE AUTHOR

Terri Kelly is Go Out And Learn, LLC's (GOAL), principal consultant. She is a performance-improvement expert with a master of arts degree in communications with an emphasis on human-resource management and organizational development. She has her coaching certification through iPec and the International Coach Federation (ICF). Terri has twenty years of experience delivering a wide variety of organizational development services. She offers extensive experience with a focus on developing and implementing solutions that achieve bottom line results, and she demonstrates skills and expertise in approaches that create competitive advantage with the "people asset."

www.GoOutAndLearnLLC.com

Made in the USA
Middletown, DE
01 May 2017